interactive SCIENCE

PEARSON

Glenview, Illinois • Boston, Massachusetts • Chandler, Arizona • Upper Saddle River, New Jersey

Program Authors

DON BUCKLEY, M.Sc.
Information and Communications Technology Director, The School at Columbia University, New York, New York
Mr. Buckley has been at the forefront of K–12 educational technology for nearly two decades. A founder of New York City Independent School Technologists (NYCIST) and long-time chair of New York Association of Independent Schools' annual IT conference, he has taught students on two continents and created multimedia and Internet-based instructional systems for schools worldwide.

ZIPPORAH MILLER, M.A.Ed.
Associate Executive Director for Professional Programs and Conferences, National Science Teachers Association, Arlington, Virginia
Associate executive director for professional programs and conferences at NSTA, Ms. Zipporah Miller is a former K–12 science supervisor and STEM coordinator for the Prince George's County Public School District in Maryland. She is a science education consultant who has overseen curriculum development and staff training for more than 150 district science coordinators.

MICHAEL J. PADILLA, Ph.D.
Associate Dean and Director, Eugene P. Moore School of Education, Clemson University, Clemson, South Carolina
A former middle school teacher and a leader in middle school science education, Dr. Michael Padilla has served as president of the National Science Teachers Association and as a writer of the National Science Education Standards. He is professor of science education at Clemson University. As lead author of the *Science Explorer* series, Dr. Padilla has inspired the team in developing a program that promotes student inquiry and meets the needs of today's students.

KATHRYN THORNTON, Ph.D.
Professor and Associate Dean, School of Engineering and Applied Science, University of Virginia, Charlottesville, Virginia
Selected by NASA in May 1984, Dr. Kathryn Thornton is a veteran of four space flights. She has logged over 975 hours in space, including more than 21 hours of extravehicular activity. As an author on the *Scott Foresman Science* series, Dr. Thornton's enthusiasm for science has inspired teachers around the globe.

MICHAEL E. WYSESSION, Ph.D.
Associate Professor of Earth and Planetary Science, Washington University, St. Louis, Missouri
An author on more than 50 scientific publications, Dr. Wysession was awarded the prestigious Packard Foundation Fellowship and Presidential Faculty Fellowship for his research in geophysics. Dr. Wysession is an expert on Earth's inner structure and has mapped various regions of Earth using seismic tomography. He is known internationally for his work in geoscience education and outreach.

Credits appear on page 87, which constitutes an extension of this copyright page.

ISBN-13: 978-0-328-52748-9
ISBN-10: 0-328-52748-3

22   19

Unit A
Science, Engineering, and Technology

Chapter 1

The Nature of Science

Chapter 2

Solve Problems

Unit B
Life Science

Chapter 3

Living and Nonliving Things

Chapter 4

Plants and Animals

Unit C
Earth Science

Chapter 5

Earth and Sky

Unit D
Physical Science

Chapter 6

Objects

Unit A

Science, Engineering, and Technology

Chapter 1
The Nature of Science

 What is science?

Chapter 2
Solve Problems

 How can you solve problems?

Computers can help you learn.

Name _____

Science, Engineering, and Technology

 Color a picture that shows something people made to help them go from place to place.

 Directions: Discuss the pictures with children. Then ask children to color the picture showing something people made so they can ride from place to place.

 Home Activity: Your child is going to study science and technology. Your home is filled with appliances, devices, and machines that are the result of scientific and technological advances. Point out an appliance, device, or machine in your home. Ask your child to name the item and tell what it is used for. Continue with other items.

Chapter 1

The Nature of Science

Why is she looking so closely?

THE BIG ? What is science?

myscienceonline.com

2

Name _____

What is science?

 Draw a picture in the hand lens.

Activity 2
Use with page 2.

Directions: Discuss observation as a practice of science, and talk about what the girl might see through the hand lens. Then have children draw a picture of a flower in the hand lens on this page.

Home Activity: Your child looked at Chapter 1, which tells about practices of science. One practice is to observe things and tell about them. Hold up an object, and ask your child to tell something about it. Then reverse roles with your child.

How do we observe?

You need

journal

hand lens

objects

1 Look.

2 Tell 3 things.

3 Repeat.

4 Draw.

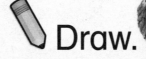

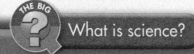

Name ____________________

Inquiry **Try It!**

How do we observe?

Draw.

Activity 3
Use with page 3.

Directions: Have children observe an object with a hand lens and draw what they see.

⊙ Picture Clues

Look at the pictures.
What do you use
to measure?
What helps you
stay safe?

Let's Read
Science!

THE BIG
?
What is science?

Name _____

Picture Clues

(Circle) what the girl can use to measure.

(Circle) what the boy can use to stay safe.

 Directions: Ask children to put their finger on the picture of the girl. Have them name each object in the row and circle the object the girl can use to measure. Repeat the process with the picture of the boy, asking children to circle the object the boy can use to stay safe.

 Home Activity: Look around your home with your child. Take turns finding things you use to measure and things you use to stay safe.

What questions can you ask?

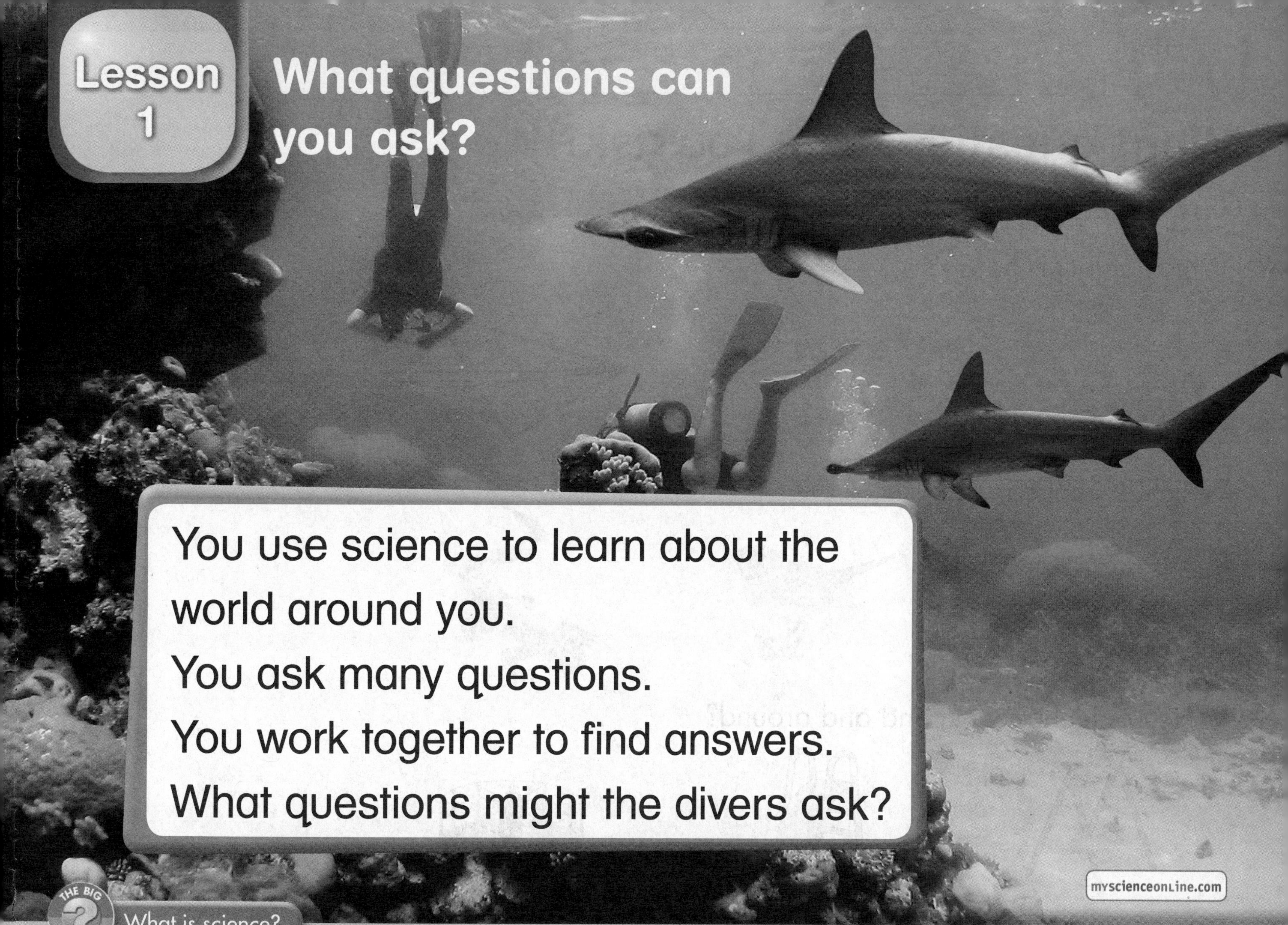

You use science to learn about the world around you.

You ask many questions.

You work together to find answers.

What questions might the divers ask?

THE BIG **?**
What is science?

What questions can you ask?

 **Circle** the picture that answers each question.

Which object is heavy?

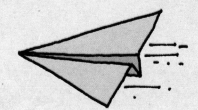

Which animal can fly?

Which object goes around and around?

 Directions: Read aloud the first question to children. Help them identify the pictures in the row. Have children choose and circle the picture that best answers the question. Ask them to explain how they figured out the answer. Repeat with the other questions.

 Home Activity: Take turns with your child, asking each other questions about objects in your home and answering them. After each question and answer, talk about what you did to figure out the answer.

How do you observe?

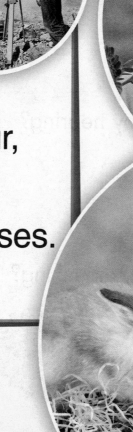

You observe the world.

You use your senses to observe.

You use your senses to look, hear, smell, touch, and taste.

These people are using their senses.

Tell what they observe.

What is science?

myscienceonline.com

Name _____

How do you observe?

Circle the pictures to answer the questions.

What can you observe by looking?

What can you observe by hearing?

What can you observe by touching?

 Directions: Read aloud the first question to children. Help them identify the pictures in the row. Have children circle the object(s) that a person can observe by looking. Ask children to explain their choice(s). Repeat with the other questions. Point out that children may have to circle more than one object in a row.

 Home Activity: Choose an object in your home. Ask your child how he or she can observe the object. If necessary, ask a question about each sense—looking, hearing, touching, smelling, and tasting—and let your child answer. For example, ask: "Can you touch the object?"

Lesson 3

How do you learn together?

You share ideas with others.

You test your ideas.

You help each other do tests.

Together you learn new things.

These children want to learn what can soak up water best.

THE BIG

? What is science?

myscienceonline.com

7

Name _____

How do you learn together?

 Color the picture that shows children working together.

 **Directions:** Discuss the two pictures with children. Ask them what the children are doing and why. Then ask children which picture shows children working together. Have children color that picture.

 Home Activity: Plan a task with your child, such as setting the table. First, talk about the task and decide how to divide the work. Then do the task. Afterward, talk about how planning and sharing helped with the work.

How do you share what you learn?

You share what you learn.
You write and draw.
You talk and show pictures.

Water

No water

Name _____

How do you share what you learn?

Think of something that moves.

Share what you know about it.

 Draw a picture of it.

Directions: Ask children to think of something that moves. It could be an animal, an object, or a person. Explain that children will share what they know about this topic with others by drawing a picture of it. Encourage them to include as many details as possible in their picture. Have children take turns displaying their pictures and telling about them.

 Home Activity: Tell your child about something you learned today. Ask your child to tell you about something he or she learned in school today. Point out that you have both shared what you learned.

What do you use to observe?

You use tools to observe.

You use tools to measure.

You use tools to write and draw.

Tools help you learn.

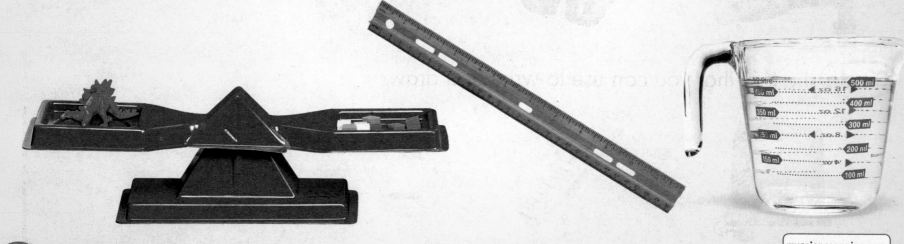

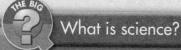

Name _____

What do you use to observe?

Circle the tool that you can use to look at things.

Circle the tool that you can use to measure.

Circle the tool that you can use to write and draw.

 Directions: Read aloud the first direction to children. Help them identify the pictures in the row. Have children choose and circle the object that they can use to look at things. Ask children to explain their choice. Repeat with the other directions.

 Home Activity: With your child, make lists of *Tools for Looking, Tools for Measuring,* and *Tools for Writing and Drawing.* Start with the tools on the page. Add other tools as you and your child think of them.

 **Activity 9**
Use with page 9.

How do you stay safe?

Rules and tools can help keep you safe.

You follow safety rules in science.

What tools help you stay safe?

Safety Rules

1. Listen to your teacher.
2. Tie your hair back.
3. Use safety tools.
4. Handle all tools carefully.
5. Wear safety goggles.
6. Wash your hands.

THE BIG ? What is science?

myscienceonline.com

How do you stay safe?

(Circle) the picture that shows a child following a science safety rule.

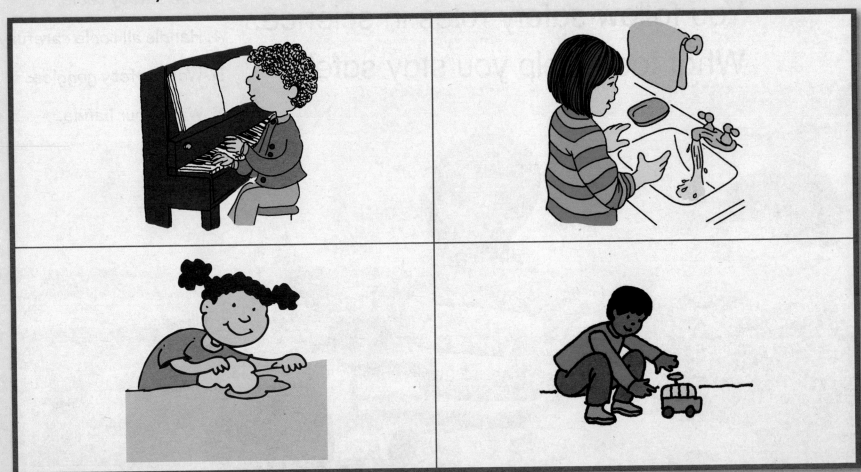

Directions: Remind children of science safety rules. Then read aloud the direction to children. Have children circle the picture showing a child following a science safety rule. Then discuss the rules depicted.

Home Activity: Talk with your child about safety rules in the home. Together make a list of rules and post the list where everyone can see it.

How do things look?

You need

journal

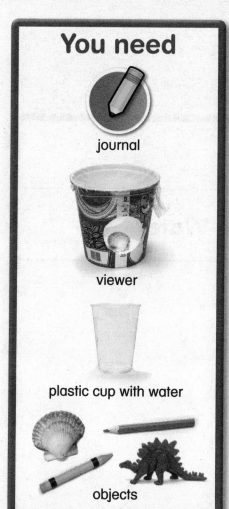

viewer

plastic cup with water

objects

1 Look.

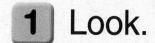 Draw.

2 Pour.

3 Look

 Draw.

Name ______________________________

Inquiry **Investigate It!**

How do things look?

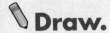

Draw.

How Things Look	
No Water	**Through Water**

Activity 11
Use with page 11.

Directions: Have children observe an object outside the viewer and then inside the viewer. Have children compare the two views.

Student Inventor

Inventors observe their world.

Inventors make things for the first time.

Christen Wooley is an inventor.

Christen was twelve years old when she invented a backpack vest.

myscienceonLine.com

Name _____

Student Inventor

(Circle) things you could carry in a backpack vest.

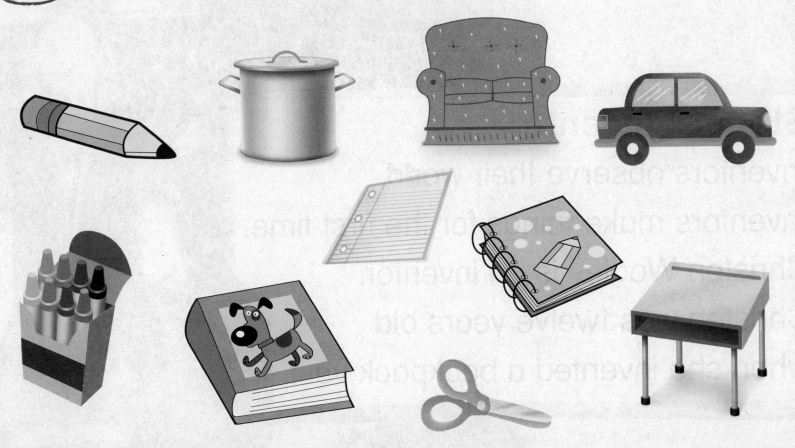

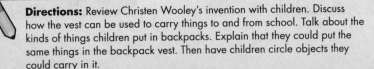

Directions: Review Christen Wooley's invention with children. Discuss how the vest can be used to carry things to and from school. Talk about the kinds of things children put in backpacks. Explain that they could put the same things in the backpack vest. Then have children circle objects they could carry in it.

Home Activity: Play a game of "put it in the backpack" with your child. Point to an object and ask your child if you can put it into a backpack. Anything can go in the backpack if it can fit inside and is not too heavy. Your child should say no to a chair but yes to a small stuffed animal, for example.

Solve Problems

How did they make the in-line skates?

 THE BIG ? How can you solve problems?

Name _____

How can you solve problems?

Circle the picture that shows in-line skates.

  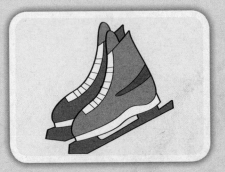

Draw a picture of someone skating with in-line skates.

 Directions: Discuss the Chapter 2 opening page. Then have children circle the pair of skates that are in-line skates. Finally, have children draw a picture of someone wearing in-line skates.

 Home Activity: Your child is studying science and technology. Show your child pictures of old and new technologies, such as telephones, cameras, and music players.

What can this object do?

You need

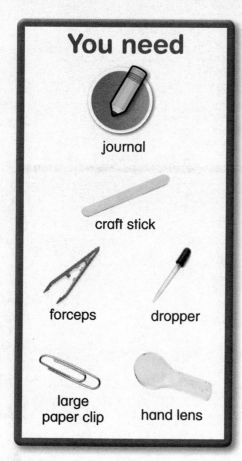

journal

craft stick

forceps

dropper

large
paper clip

hand lens

1 Look.

2 Choose.

Draw.

3 Tell.

4 Compare.

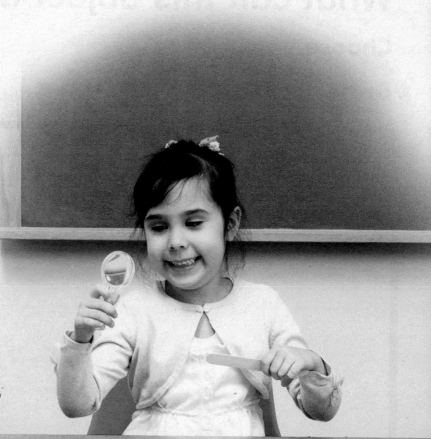

THE BIG

How can you solve problems?

Name ____

Inquiry **Try It!**

What can this object do?

Choose.

Draw.

Activity 14
Use with page 14.

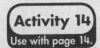

Directions: Have children use the hand lens to look at the forceps, dropper, craft stick, and paper clip. Then have children draw what they see.

⊙ **Cause and Effect**

What made the light turn on?

THE BIG
?

How can you solve problems?

myscienceonLine.com

Cause and Effect

Look at what happened in each row.

Circle the picture that shows why it happened.

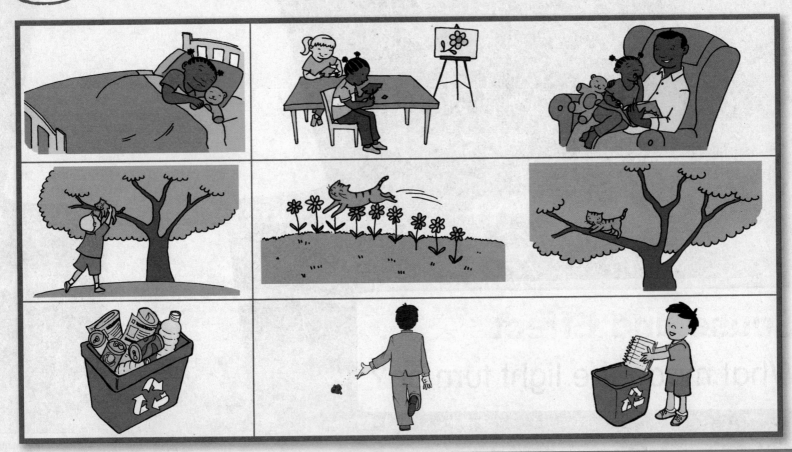

Directions: Tell children that the first picture in each row shows what has happened. Have children tell what they see in the first picture in row 1. Then have children circle the picture that shows why the girl is asleep in bed. Continue the same way for rows 2 and 3.

Home Activity: Help children point out cause-and-effect relationships in their everyday lives. For example, your teeth are clean and healthy because you brush them.

What problem can you solve?

You might spill when you drink from a glass.

This is a problem.

A straw is the solution.

Many straws are plastic.

THE BIG ? How can you solve problems?

myscienceonline.com

Name _____

What problem can you solve?

Look at the problem in the first picture.

(Circle) a solution to the problem.

Directions: Help children identify the problem shown in the first picture in the first row. Ask them to circle a possible solution to the problem. Repeat the procedure for the second row.

Home Activity: Identify simple household problems, such as dirty dishes or dry plants. Ask your child to help you identify a way to solve the problem and then help you carry out the solution.

How can you make a plan?

You plan how to make a straw.

You write and draw.

You make the straw.

It works!

THE BIG How can you solve problems?

myscienceonline.com

17

Name _____

How can you make a plan?

Think of a something you would like to make with connecting blocks.

 Draw a plan. Show what you want to make.

Directions: Tell children that a plan shows what to make or how to make it. Then tell children to draw something they could make with connecting blocks. Encourage them to use the blocks to make what their plans show.

Home Activity: Talk with your child about plans you use or make. You may use recipes in the kitchen or draw up a list of errands. You may follow plans for putting together a toy or piece of furniture. Show the plans to your child and tell how you use them.

You show your drawing.
You tell about the straw.
Others can use the straw too.

Name _____

How can you share your ideas with others?

(Circle) the picture of a person sharing information.

Activity 18
Use with page 18.

Directions: Discuss with children how they can share ideas and information with others. Then have children circle the picture showing someone sharing information.

Home Activity: Draw a picture of something you plan to do tomorrow, such as walk your child to school or make dinner. Share your picture with your child and discuss what it shows.

How can you lift heavy things?

You need

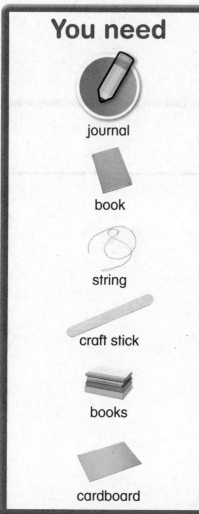

journal

book

string

craft stick

books

cardboard

1 Tie.

2 Put.

3 Pull.

4 Put.

5 Push.

6 Write.

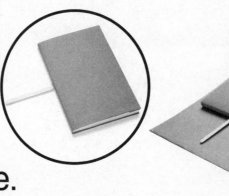

How can you solve problems?

Name ____________________

Inquiry **Investigate It!**

How can you lift heavy things?

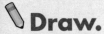

Draw.

Pull	Push

Directions: Have children draw how they pull the book up the ramp and how they push the book up the ramp.

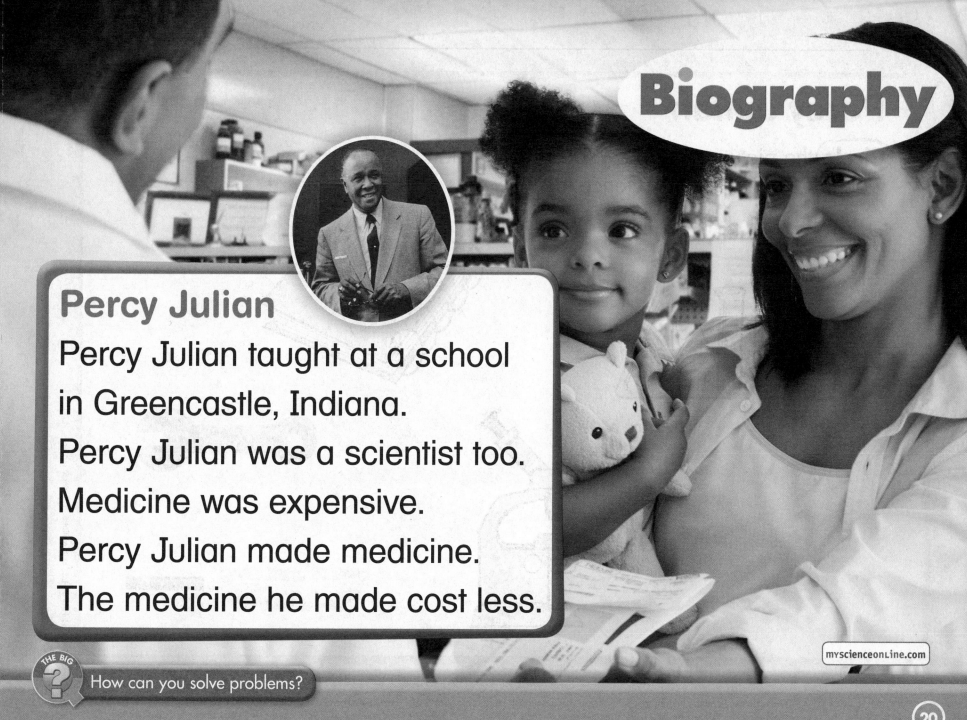

Percy Julian

Percy Julian taught at a school in Greencastle, Indiana.

Percy Julian was a scientist too.

Medicine was expensive.

Percy Julian made medicine.

The medicine he made cost less.

THE BIG ? How can you solve problems?

mYscienceonLine.com

20

Percy Julian

(Circle) the pictures that show tools Percy Julian would have used in his science lab.

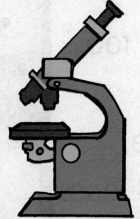

Activity 20
Use with page 20.

Directions: Remind children that Percy Julian was a scientist. Help them recall the tools a scientist uses. Then ask them to circle the tools Percy Julian might have used in his work as a scientist.

Home Activity: Your child learned about Percy Julian, a teacher and scientist. Ask your child to tell you about the tools scientists use in their work.

How can you make a maze?

You need

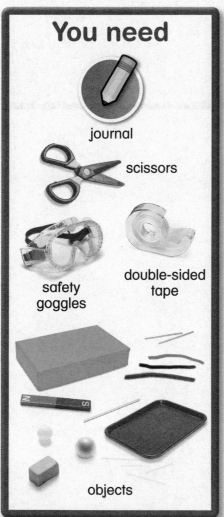

journal

scissors

safety goggles

double-sided tape

objects

1 Plan.

2 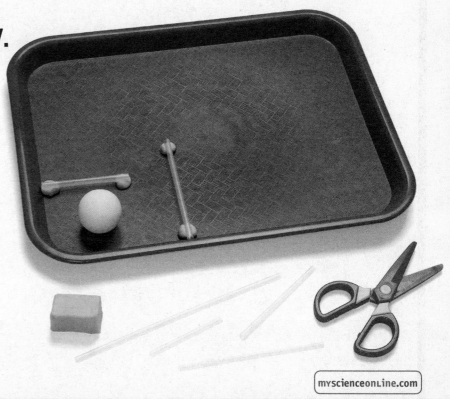 Draw.

3 Make.

4 Test.

Inquiry | **Design It!**

How can you make a maze?

 Draw.

Directions: Have children draw their maze before they begin to make it.

Life Science

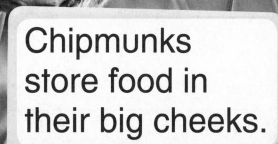

Chipmunks store food in their big cheeks.

Name _____

Life Science

 Draw a plant.

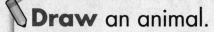 **Draw** an animal.

Activity 22
Use with page 22.

Directions: Discuss plants and animals, asking children to name different kinds of plants and animals. Then have children draw a plant and an animal. Have them tell about the plant and the animal they drew.

Home Activity: In science, your child is learning about living things. Together with your child, look through a picture book and ask your child to point to living things and identify them as plants or animals.

Living and Nonliving Things

Which is living?

What can you tell about living things?

myscienceonline.com

Name _____

What can you tell about living things?

Look at the bears.

(Circle) two bears that look like living bears.

Directions: Help children distinguish features of toy bears and living bears. Then have children circle the two bears on the page that look most like real bears.

Home Activity: With your child, gather and sort pictures of living animals and toy or cartoon animals. Talk about how you can tell the difference between the real animals and the toy or cartoon animals.

What things are living?

You need

journal

objects

1 Look.

2 Tell.

3 Draw.

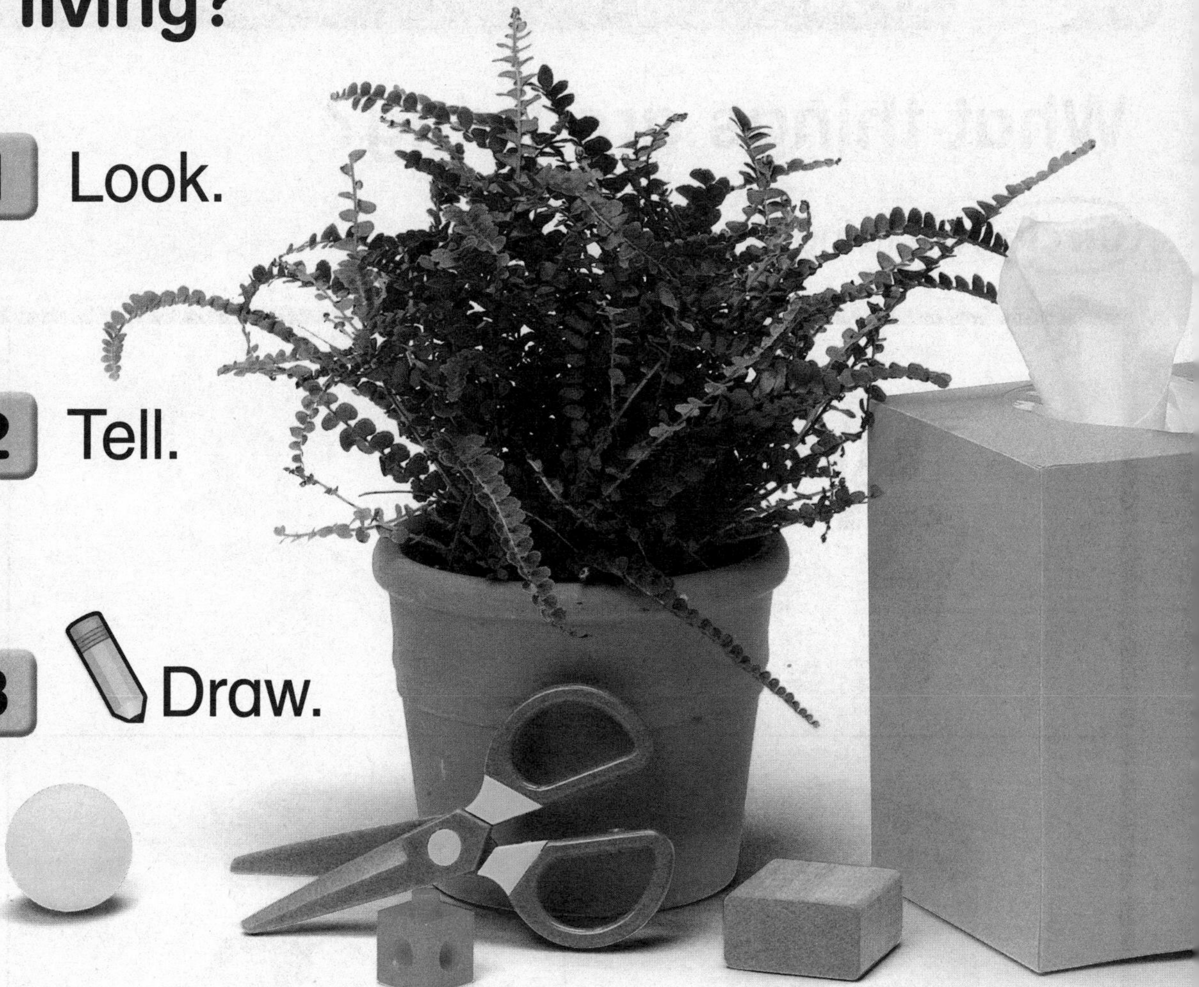

THE BIG ? What can you tell about living things?

Name _____

What things are living?

 two living things.

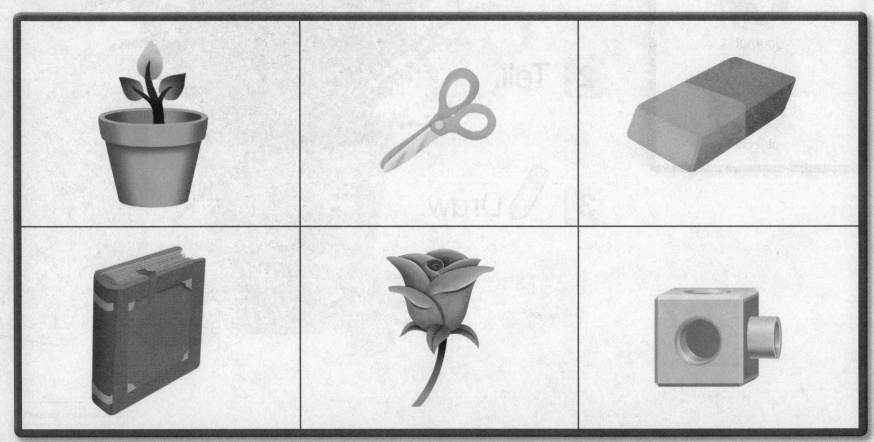

 Directions: Have children circle the pictures of two living things.

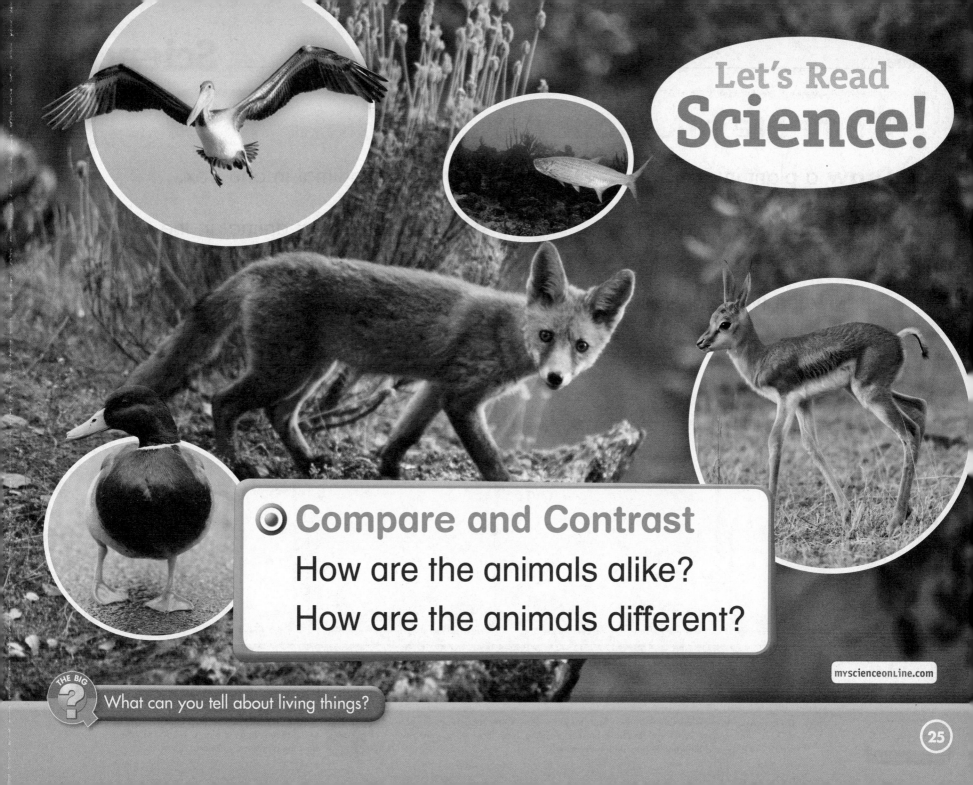

⦿ **Compare and Contrast**

How are the animals alike?

How are the animals different?

myscienceonLine.com

THE BIG ? What can you tell about living things?

Compare and Contrast

 **Draw** a plant in one box.

Draw a different plant in the other box.

Tell how the two plants are alike.

 **Draw** an animal in one box.

Draw a different animal in the other box.

Tell how the two animals are alike.

 Directions: Have children think of two plants they can draw. Offer suggestions or show pictures, if necessary. When children have finished drawing, have them tell how their two plants are alike and different. Repeat with two animals.

 Home Activity: Show your child pictures of two different kinds of plants. Take turns telling how the plants are alike and different.

Nonliving things do not grow.

Nonliving things do not change or move on their own.

Look around.

You will see many nonliving things.

THE BIG ？ What can you tell about living things?

Name _____

What are nonliving things?

Circle the nonliving thing in each row.

 Directions: Help children identify the pictures in each row. Then have them circle the picture that shows a nonliving thing.

 Home Activity: Point out living and nonliving things in your environment, such as a tree and a stop sign. Ask your child which is the nonliving thing.

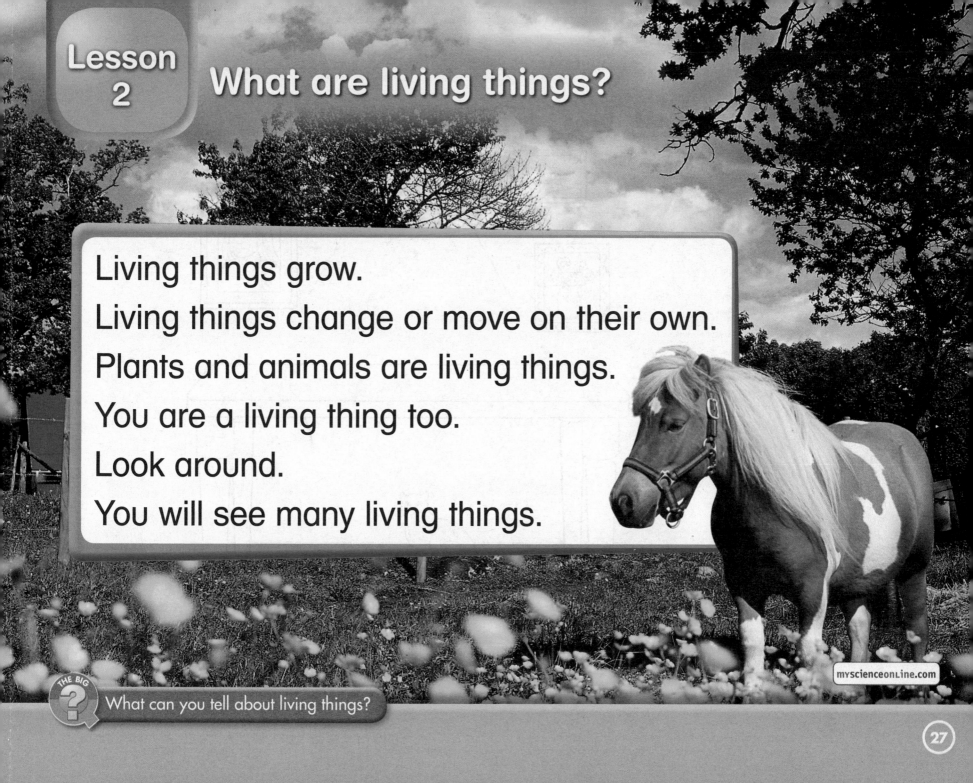

Living things grow.

Living things change or move on their own.

Plants and animals are living things.

You are a living thing too.

Look around.

You will see many living things.

THE BIG ? What can you tell about living things?

myscienceonline.com

Name _____

What are living things?

(**Circle**) the two living things in the picture.

Color the picture.

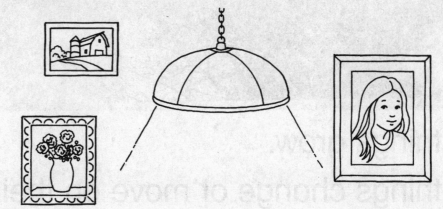

Directions: Discuss with children how living things differ from nonliving things. Then ask children to circle the two living things in the picture. Encourage children to color the picture.

Home Activity: Help your child identify living things in and around your home.

What do living things need?

All living things have needs.

Living things need space and air.

Living things need water and food.

You are a living thing.

What do you need?

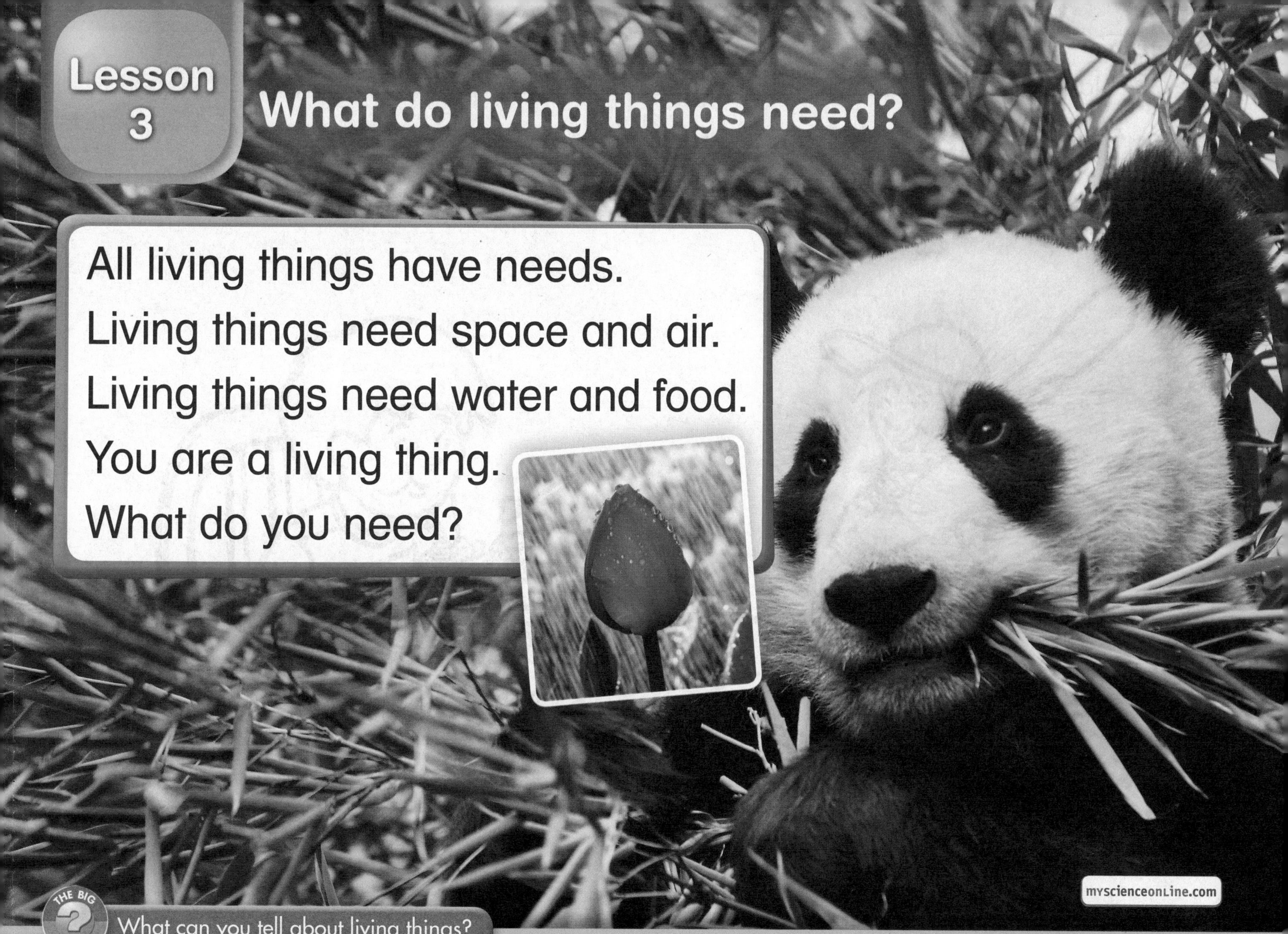

myscienceonline.com

28

Name _____

What do living things need?

 Color the picture of the boy meeting a need.

 Activity 28
Use with page 28.

Directions: Ask children to color the picture that shows the boy doing something he needs to do to live.

 Home Activity: Let your child help you water a plant, feed a pet, or pour a glass of juice. Talk about how living things need food, water, air, and space to live.

Lesson 4

How are animals alike and different?

Animals have different colors and shapes.

Animals have different body coverings.

Animals have different ways of moving.

Tell about the animals in the pictures.

How are they alike?

THE BIG ? What can you tell about living things?

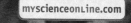

Name _____

How are animals alike and different?

 Circle the two animals that move alike.

Circle the animal that has fur or hair.

Circle the animal that does not have legs.

 **Directions:** Help children identify the pictures in the first row. Repeat the process for the pictures in the second and third rows.

 Home Activity: Identify features of animals you and your child see. For example, if you see a dog, note that it moves by walking and running, its body is covered with fur, and so on.

Lesson 5 How are plants alike and different?

Plants can be different shapes, sizes, and colors. Plants can feel rough or smooth. Tell about the plants in the picture. Tell how they might feel.

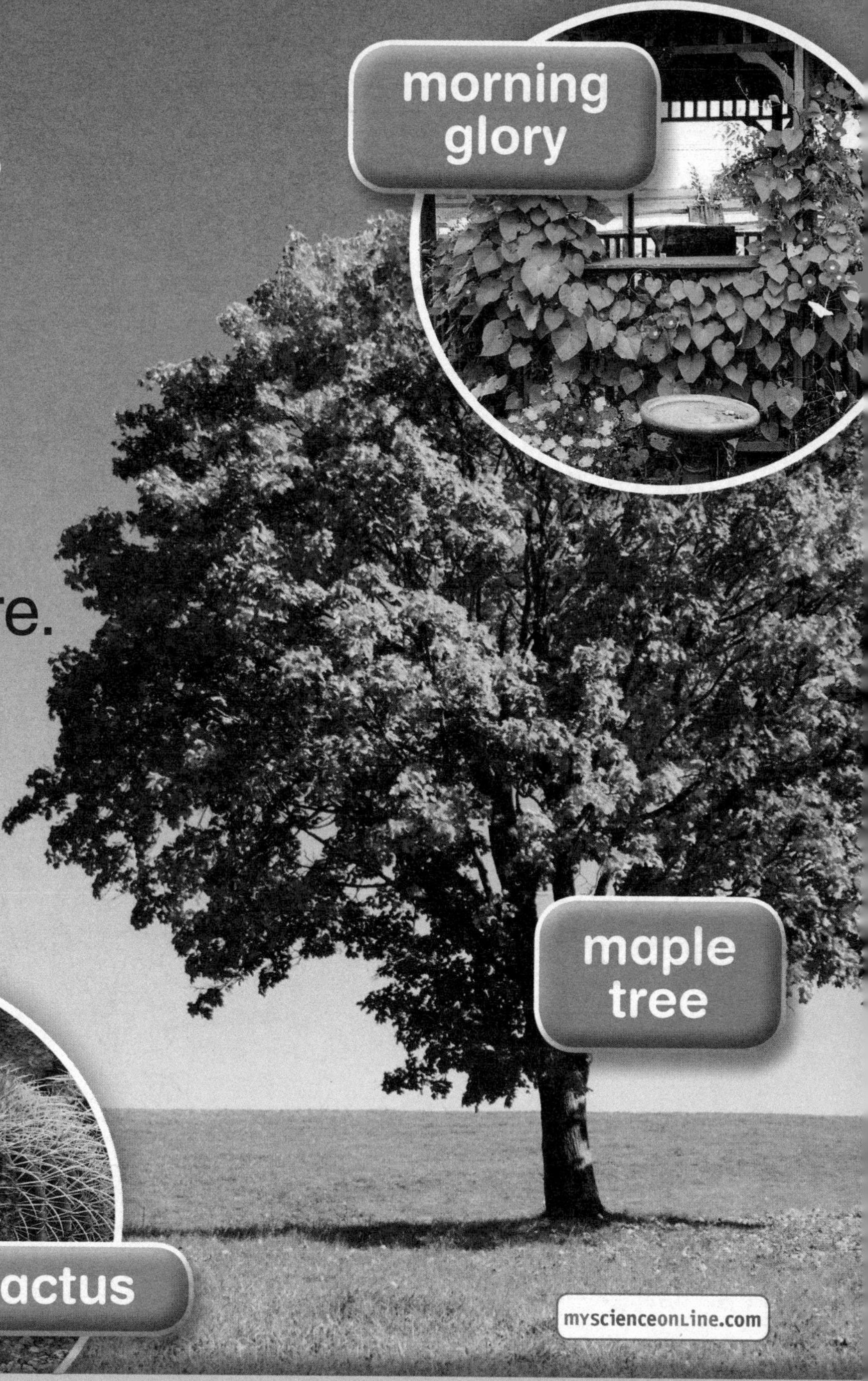
morning glory
maple tree

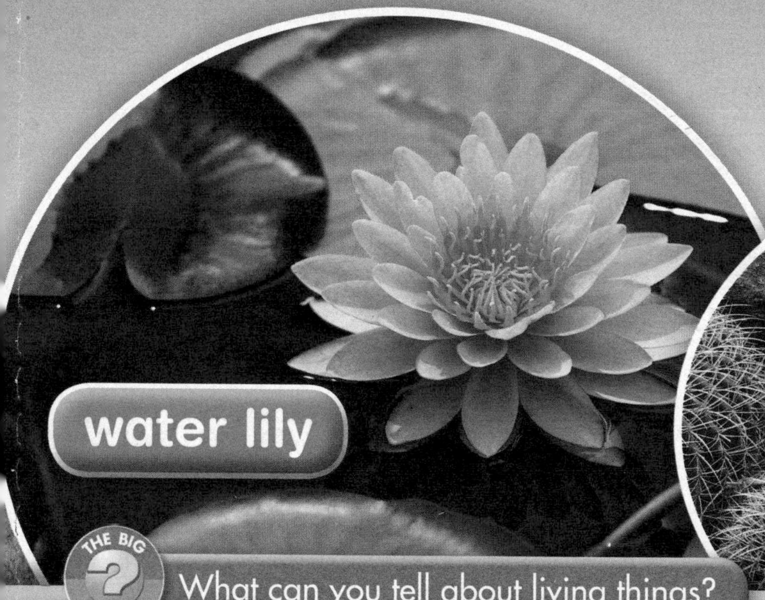
water lily

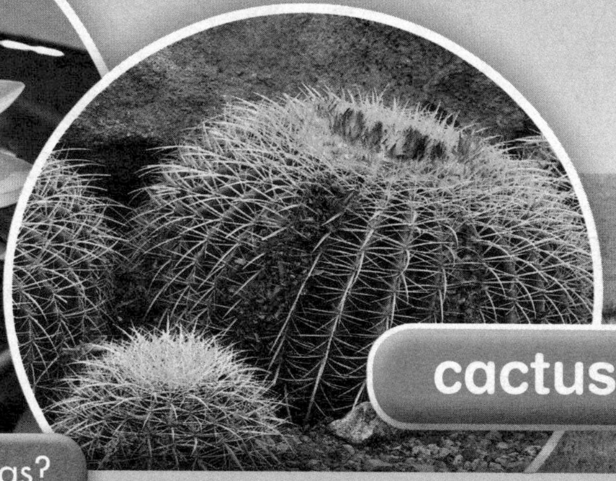
cactus

mysciencEonLine.com

THE BIG ? What can you tell about living things?

How are plants alike and different?

Color the tree trunk and branch brown.

Color leaves green.

Color the flower red.

Draw an X on a plant part that feels rough.

Circle a plant part that feels smooth.

Activity 30
Use with page 30.

Directions: Read the directions to children and have them color the parts of the picture as directed. Then have them draw an X on a rough plant part and circle a smooth plant part.

Home Activity: If possible, feel plant parts with your child and talk about the textures. Tree trunks may feel rough whereas flowers may feel smooth.

How are animals and plants different?

You need

journal

1 Look.

2  Write.

3 Compare.

4 Tell.

Dog

Bird

Tree

Daisy Plant

THE BIG ?

What can you tell about living things?

Name _____

How are animals and plants different?

 Draw.

Dog	Bird
Tree	**Daisy Plant**

Activity 31
Use with page 31.

 Directions: Have children look at the images of the dog, bird, tree, and daisy plant in the Investigate It activity. Then have children draw pictures that show the features of each living thing.

Living and Nonliving Things

Living and nonliving things can be found almost everywhere.

Look around you.

What living things do you see?

What nonliving things do you see?

THE BIG ? What can you tell about living things?

myscienceonline.com

Name _____

Living and Nonliving Things

(Circle) pictures of living things.

Activity 32
Use with page 32.

 Directions: Identify each picture in the box. Then have children circle the pictures of living things.

 Home Activity: As you walk with your child, take turns identifying living and nonliving things.

Chapter

4

Plants and Animals

What are these?

THE BIG ? How do living things change as they grow?

Name _____

How do living things change as they grow?

Circle the small picture that shows the kind of animal you see in the large picture.

Color the large picture.

Activity 33
Use with page 33.

Directions: Point to and name the animals in the small pictures. Then have children look at the large picture. Tell children to circle the small picture that shows the same kind of animal. Then have them color the large picture.

Home Activity: Show your child pictures of animals and help your child name each animal.

How do seeds change?

You need

journal

beans

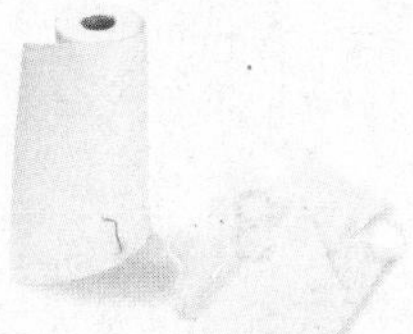

paper towel

resealable plastic bag

1 Look.

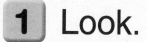 **2**  Draw.

3 Tell.

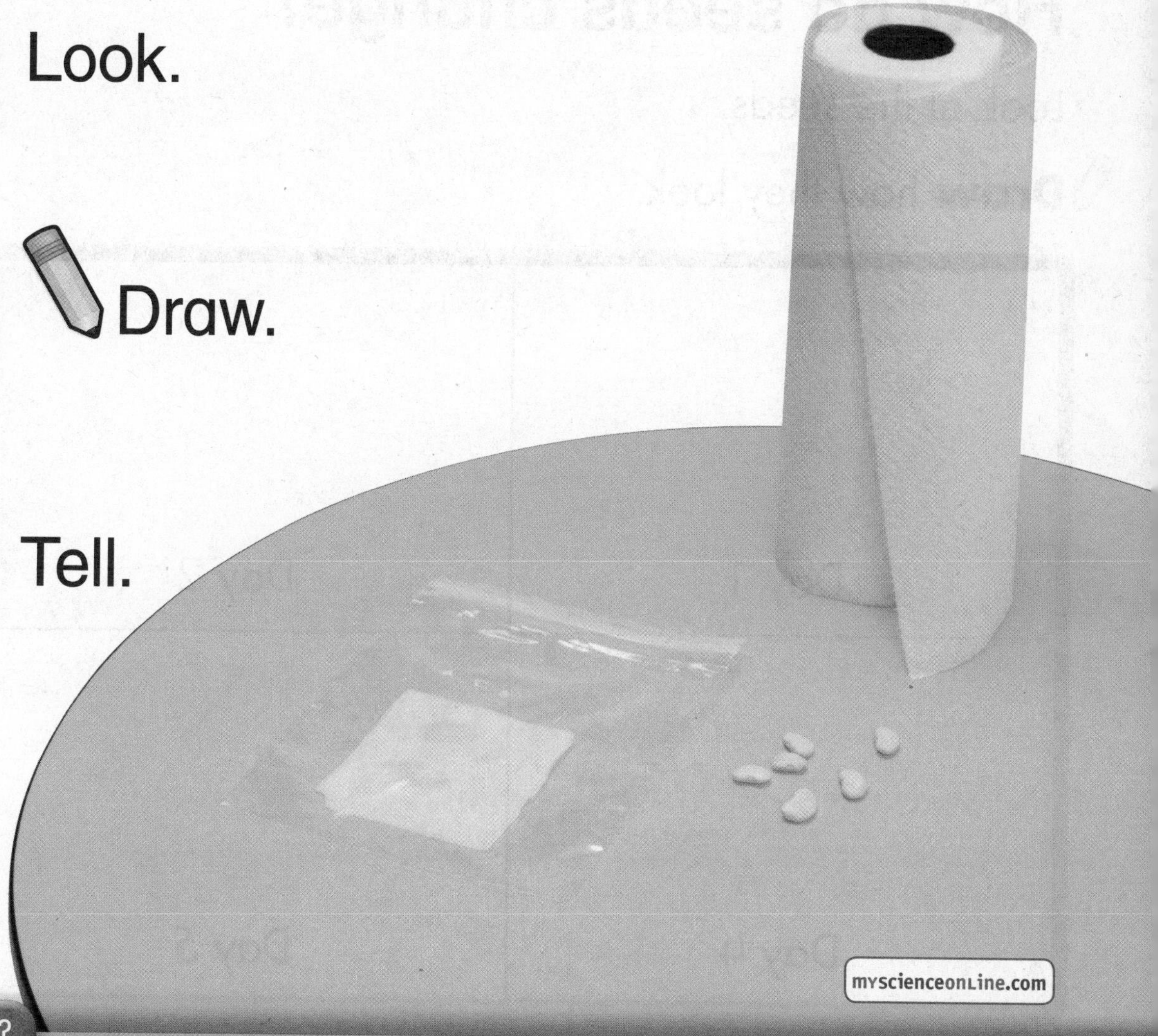

Name _____

How do seeds change?

Look at the seeds.

 Draw how they look.

Day 1	Day 2	Day 3
Day 4	Day 5	Day 6

Activity 34
Use with page 34.

 Directions: Put the seed in a glass of water and have children observe it for six days. Tell them to draw what the seed looks like each day and tell how the seed's appearance has changed.

Sequence

The egg comes first.

Which comes second?

Which comes third?

Which comes next?

Which comes last?

Let's Read
Science!

myscienceonline.com

THE BIG ? How do living things change as they grow?

Name _____

Sequence

 Write a number to show the order.

1

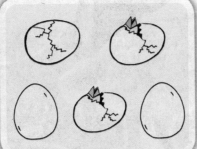

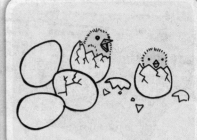

Activity 35
Use with page 35.

Directions: Tell children to number the pictures in the order that the eggs hatch and the chicks become adults. Number 1 has been done for children.

Home Activity: Your child has learned about sequence of events. Read a story with your child. Ask questions about the sequence of events. For example, ask: "What happened first?" "Then what happened?"

How are young animals like their parents?

butterfly

Animals grow and change.
Some babies look like their parents.
Some babies do not look like
their parents.
The babies change as they grow.

kitten

gosling

caterpillar

goose

calf

whale

cat

myscienceonline.com

THE BIG ? How do living things change as they grow?

Name _____

How are young animals like their parents?

 **Draw** a line to connect each picture of a baby animal with the picture of its parent.

 Directions: Help children identify the baby names of the animals—cub (bear), calf (whale), puppy (dog), and cub (lion). Then have children draw lines to match the babies with their parents.

 Home Activity: Find pictures of baby animals and adult animals. Help your child match the pictures of the babies and adults.

How do animals change?

Animals can change and grow in different ways.

A tadpole is a baby frog.

A tadpole changes and grows.

A puppy is a baby dog.

A puppy changes and grows.

egg

tadpole

young frog

frog

newborn puppy

dog

older puppy

myscienceonLine.com

THE BIG

How do living things change as they grow?

37

Name _____

How do animals change?

 **Draw** arrows to show how frogs grow and change.

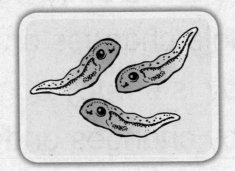

 Directions: Discuss with children how frogs change as they grow and develop. Then have children draw arrows to show the development of a frog. You might ask questions to guide children as they complete the activity.

 Home Activity: Ask your child to use this page to show and explain how frogs grow and change.

Activity 37
Use with page 37.

How do plants change?

Many plants grow from seeds.

A tree is a plant.

A tree changes and grows.

A daisy is a plant.

A daisy changes and grows.

seed

seedling

tree

seed

seedling

daisy

THE BIG

How do living things change as they grow?

Name _____

How do plants change?

 Draw a seed in the first flowerpot.

Draw a seedling in the next pot.

Draw a flower in the last pot.

 Directions: Ask children to draw a seed in the first flowerpot, a seedling in the second flowerpot, and a plant with a flower in the third flowerpot. Have children use their drawings to help explain how plants change and grow.

 Home Activity: Cut out or draw pictures of seeds, seedlings, and flowering plants. Have your child glue the pictures in a circle and draw arrows to show the cycle of plant growth.

Activity 38
Use with page 38.

How do people change?

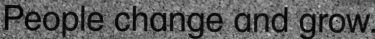

People change and grow.

You grow and get bigger.

The way you look changes.

The things you can do change.

Tell how you are different from a baby.

THE BIG ?

What can you tell about living things?

Name _____

How do people change?

 Write numbers to show how people grow and change.

_____   _ _ _ _ _ _ _   _____   _ _ _ _ _ _ _

_____   _ _ _ _ _ _ _   _____   _____

 Activity 39
Use with page 39.

 Directions: Have children look at the pictures on this page. Ask which picture shows the person when he was a tiny baby. Have children number that picture 1. Tell them to continue numbering the pictures to show how people change from baby to adult.

Home Activity: Look at old pictures of your child. Talk about how your child has changed over time.

Different plants and animals live in different places.

Some plants and animals live on land.

Plants and animals get what they need where they live.

Name _____

What are some plants and animals that live on land?

(Circle) plants and animals that live on land.

 Directions: Remind children that plants and animals get what they need where they live. Talk with children about what the plants and animals in the pictures need. Talk about what characteristics plants and animals that live on land need. Then have children circle plants and animals that live on land.

 Home Activity: Go outside with your child and look around. Discuss plants and animals you see. Talk about which plants and animals live on land.

What are some plants and animals that live in water?

Some plants and animals live in water. These plants and animals get what they need in water.

Tell about plants and animals that live in water.

Name _____

What are some plants and animals that live in water?

 Draw plants and animals that live in water.

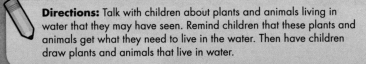 **Directions:** Talk with children about plants and animals living in water that they may have seen. Remind children that these plants and animals get what they need to live in the water. Then have children draw plants and animals that live in water.

 Home Activity: Look at pictures with children of plants and animals living in water. Ask children what these plants and animals need to live. Talk with children about how they get what they need in the water where they live.

How does a butterfly change?

You need

journal

caterpillars

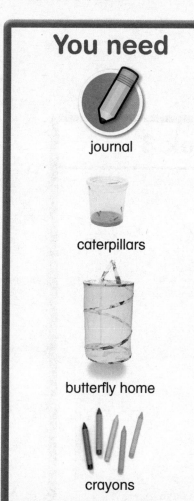

butterfly home

crayons

1 Look.

Draw.

2 Wait.
Look.
Draw.

3 Wait.
Look.
Draw.

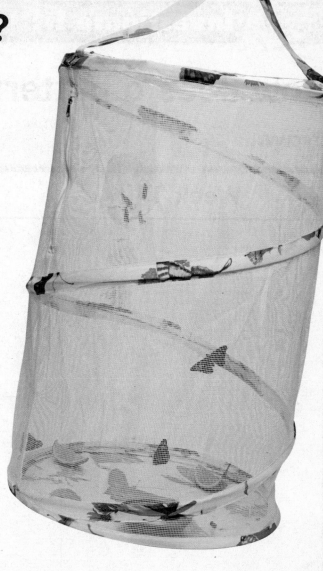

 THE BIG ? How do living things change as they grow?

myscienceonLine.com

42

Name _____

How does a butterfly change?

 Draw.

Week 1	Week 2	Week 3

 **Directions:** Have children look in the butterfly home every day for 3 weeks. Have them draw what they see each week to record the changes from caterpillar to chrysalis to butterfly.

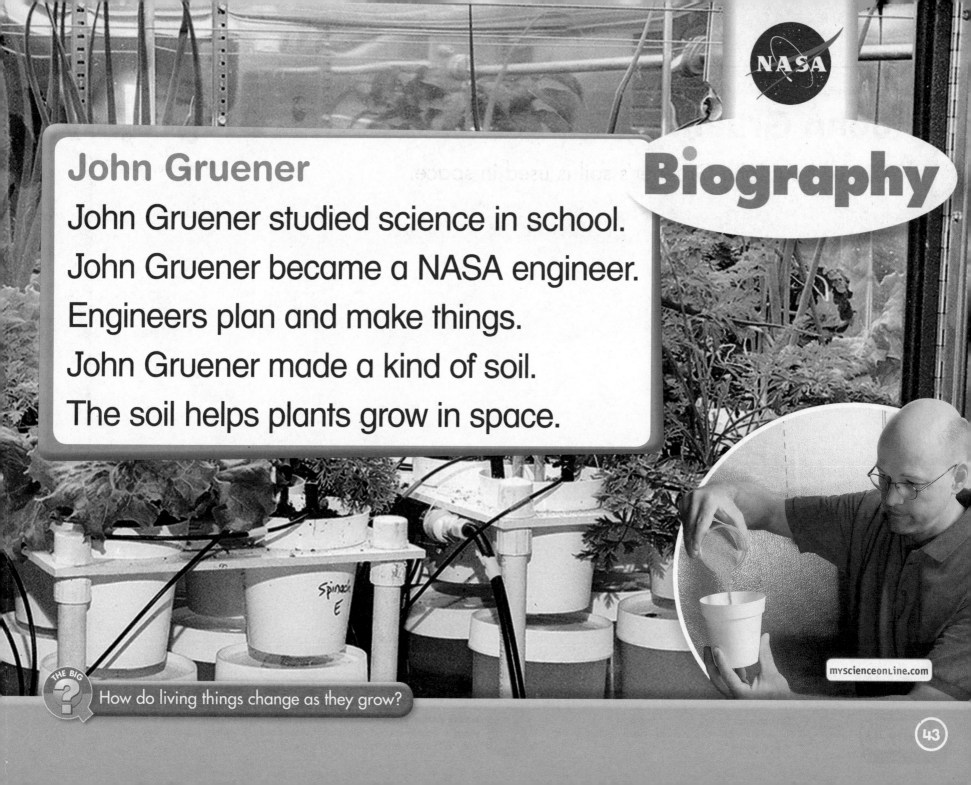

Biography

John Gruener

John Gruener studied science in school.

John Gruener became a NASA engineer.

Engineers plan and make things.

John Gruener made a kind of soil.

The soil helps plants grow in space.

THE BIG
?
How do living things change as they grow?

mYscienceonLine.com

Name _____

John Gruener

 Draw how John Gruener's soil is used in space.

 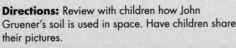 **Directions:** Review with children how John Gruener's soil is used in space. Have children share their pictures.

 Home Activity: Your child has learned about how living things grow and change. Help your child plant and care for a seed. Watch as it grows. Talk with your child about the changes you observe.

Earth Science

Chapter 5
Earth and Sky

THE BIG ? What are Earth and the sky like?

The weather is usually warm in summer.

Name _____

Earth Science

 Draw the sky.

Show the sun.

Activity 44
Use with page 44.

Directions: Tell children that in science you learn about the world around you. You can learn about the sky. Have children look out a classroom window at the sky, or take them outside to look at the sky. Remind them not to look directly at the sun. Ask them to draw a daytime sky with the sun in it. Encourage them to add something else they might see in the daytime sky.

Home Activity: Your child is learning about the sky, the seasons, and weather. With your child, look in picture books or magazines for pictures of the sky. Talk about what you see in the sky in each picture.

Earth and Sky

Is it night or day?

THE BIG ? — What are Earth and the sky like?

myscienceonline.com

Name _____

What are Earth and sky like?

Look at the pictures.

Color the picture that shows what the chapter is about.

 Directions: Then have children color the picture on this page that shows what Chapter 5 is about.

 Home Activity: In Chapter 5, your child will learn about the sky and the objects that can be seen in the sky. Take time to look at the daytime sky with your child. Talk about what you see. Do you see clouds, the sun, airplanes, or birds?

How does weather change?

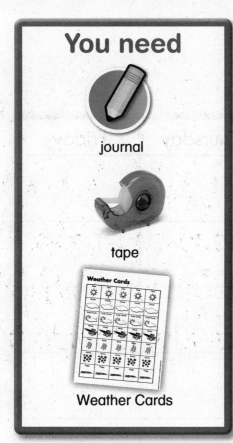

You need

journal

tape

Weather Cards

1 Observe the weather.

2 Record.

3 Count.

	Monday	Tuesday	Wednesday	Thursday	Friday
Clear					
Cloudy					
Partly cloudy					
Windy					
Rainy or snowy					
Foggy					

THE BIG ? What are Earth and the sky like?

Name _____

How does weather change?

🖊 **Record.**

	Monday	Tuesday	Wednesday	Thursday	Friday
Clear ☀️					
Cloudy ☁️					
Partly Cloudy ⛅					
Rainy or snowy 🌧❄️					
Windy 🌬					
Foggy 🌫					

 Directions: Have children check the box for the type of weather they see each day. Have them record the weather each week for one month.

Draw Conclusions

What was the weather like here?

How do you know?

THE BIG

? What are Earth and the sky like?

myscienceonline.com

Draw Conclusions

Look at the picture of a place on Earth.

(Circle) the picture that tells what the weather is usually like in this place.

Directions: Discuss the place shown in the large picture. Then ask children to use what they know and the picture to draw conclusions about the weather in this place. Have children circle the small picture that shows what the weather is like.

Home Activity: Help your child practice drawing conclusions using weather-specific clothing, such as raincoats, mittens, shorts, umbrellas, and sweaters. Display the clothing and ask your child when he or she would wear it and why.

Earth has water and land.
Water covers most of Earth.
Tell about the water and land
on Earth.

Earth

bayou

plains

river

ocean

swamp

mountains

Name _____

What makes up Earth?

 Draw a line to match each word with the correct picture.

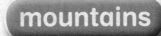

river   plains   mountains   ocean

 Directions: Read the words to children. Help them identify the pictures. Discuss which picture goes with each word. Have children draw lines to match the words with the appropriate pictures.

 Home Activity: Look through books or magazines for pictures of lakes, rivers, oceans, swamps, plains, and mountains. Help your child name each landform and body of water shown.

You can see clouds and the sun in the day sky.
Sometimes you can see the moon in the day sky.
Tell about objects in the day sky.

THE BIG ?
What are Earth and the sky like?

mYscienceonLine.com

49

What can you see in the day sky?

(Circle) the objects you might see in the day sky.

 Directions: Have children identify each picture. Then have children circle the objects they can see in the sky during the day. Review the page, emphasizing that sometimes the moon can be seen in the day sky and sometimes it can be seen in the night sky. Ask which object is never seen in the sky.

 Home Activity: Your child identified things that can be seen in the daytime sky. Together with your child, discuss what you would see in the daytime sky. Then draw a picture of the objects in the sky.

Lesson 3 How does the sun seem to move?

The sun looks low in the morning sky.
The sun looks high in the sky at noon.
The sun looks low in the evening sky.

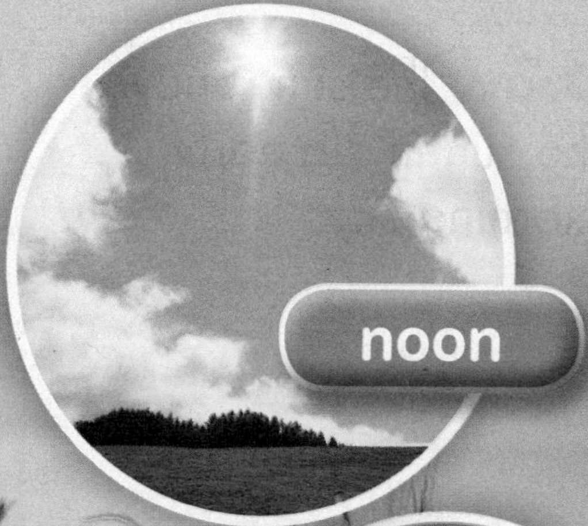
noon

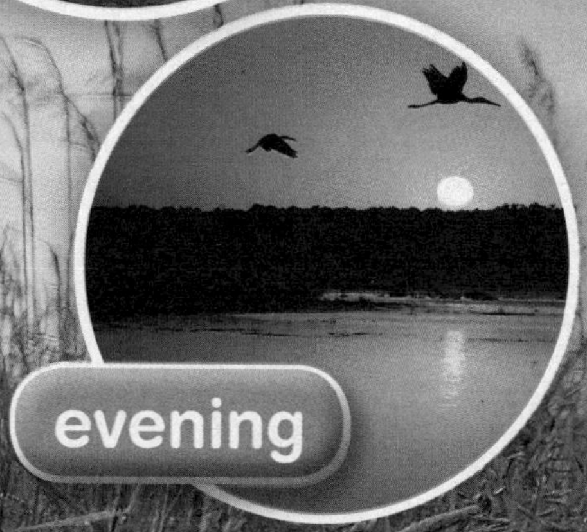
evening

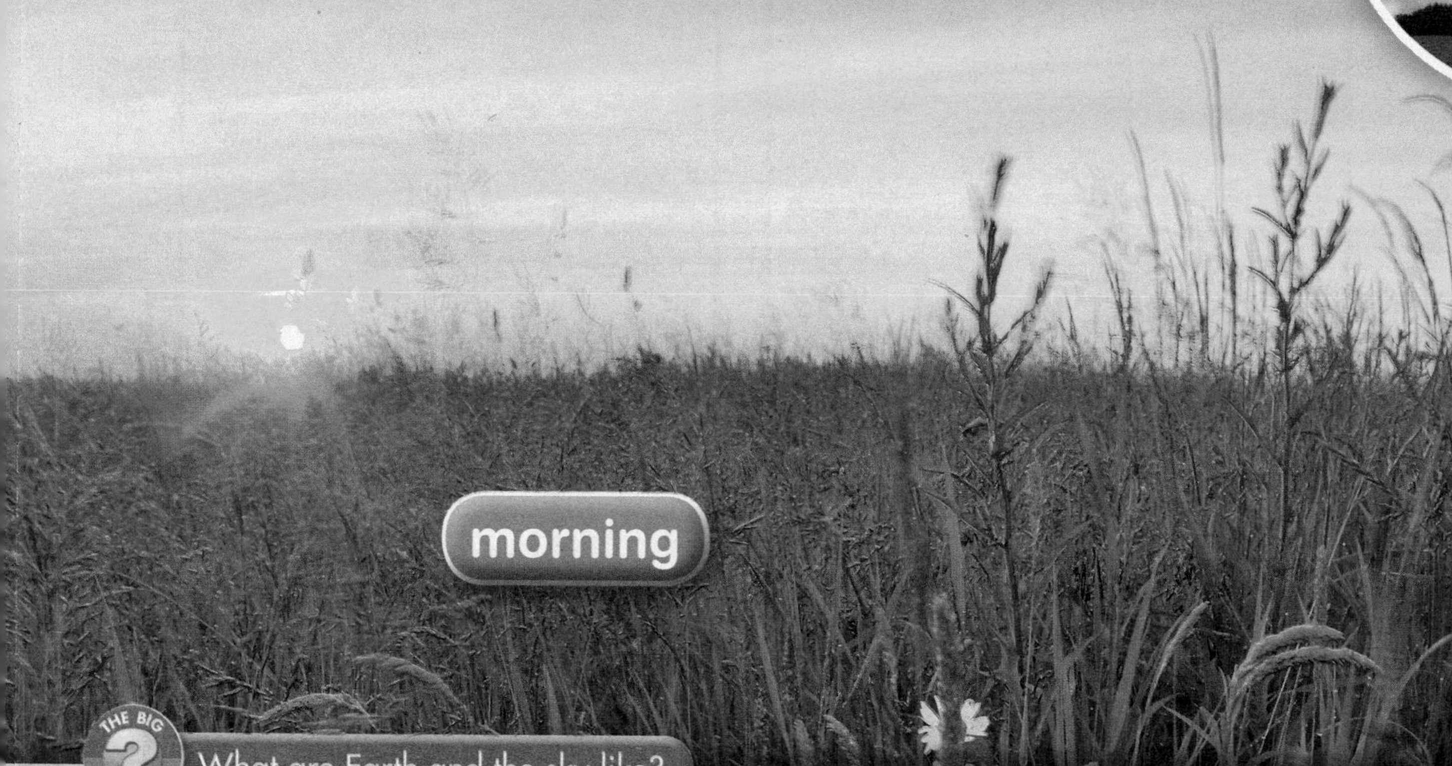
morning
myscienceonline.com

THE BIG ? What are Earth and the sky like?

Name _____

How does the sun seem to move?

✏ **Draw** the sun. Show the sun in the early morning sky.

✏ **Draw** the sun. Show the sun in the sky at noon.

✏ **Draw** the sun. Show the sun in the early evening sky.

Activity 50
Use with page 50.

✏ **Directions:** Read the directions for the first picture to children. Help them identify where to draw the sun. Then have them draw the sun. Repeat the process for the second and third pictures.

 Home Activity: Together with your child look at the sky at different times of day. Draw pictures showing where the sun is at each time. Write the time on each picture.

What can you see in the night sky?

You can see stars in the night sky.
Sometimes you can see the moon in the night sky.
Sometimes you can see clouds too.
Tell how objects in the day and night sky are alike.

THE BIG
? What are Earth and the sky like?

myscienceonline.com

Name _____

What can you see in the night sky?

What can you see in the night sky?

Circle the objects you might see in the night sky.

Draw a picture of the night sky.

Show the objects you circled.

Activity 51
Use with page 51.

Directions: Ask children to identify each picture and to circle the objects that can be seen in the night sky. Then have children draw a picture of the night sky that includes the circled objects.

Home Activity: Your child identified things that can be seen in a nighttime sky. With your child, draw a picture of a nighttime sky. Talk about what you can see in the nighttime sky that you cannot see in the daytime sky.

What are some kinds of weather?

The weather can change every day.

The weather may be sunny, cloudy, windy, rainy, or snowy.

You can show the weather on a calendar.

Show what the weather is like today.

April

Sunday	Monday	Tuesday	Wednesday	Thursday	Friday	Saturday
				1	2	3
4	5	6	7	8	9	10
11	12	13	14	15	16	17
18	19	20	21	22	23	24
25	26	27	28	29	30	

myscienceonline.com

THE BIG ? What are Earth and the sky like?

Name _____

What are some kinds of weather?

 Color the picture that best shows what the weather is like today.

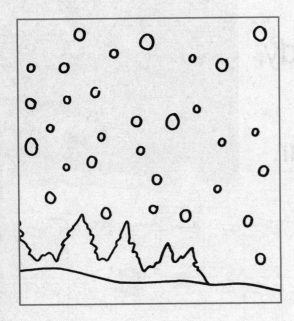

Activity 52
Use with page 52.

 Directions: Look at the pictures with children. Discuss the type of weather each picture shows and the weather children observed today. Then have them color the picture that best matches today's weather.

Home Activity: Discuss these kinds of weather with your child: sunny, cloudy, windy, rainy, and snowy. Have your child draw a picture of himself or herself outdoors in today's weather.

Lesson 6

What are the seasons?

The seasons may have different kinds of weather.
Summer may be hot.
Fall may be cool.
Winter may be cold.
Spring may be warm.
Tell about the seasons where you live.

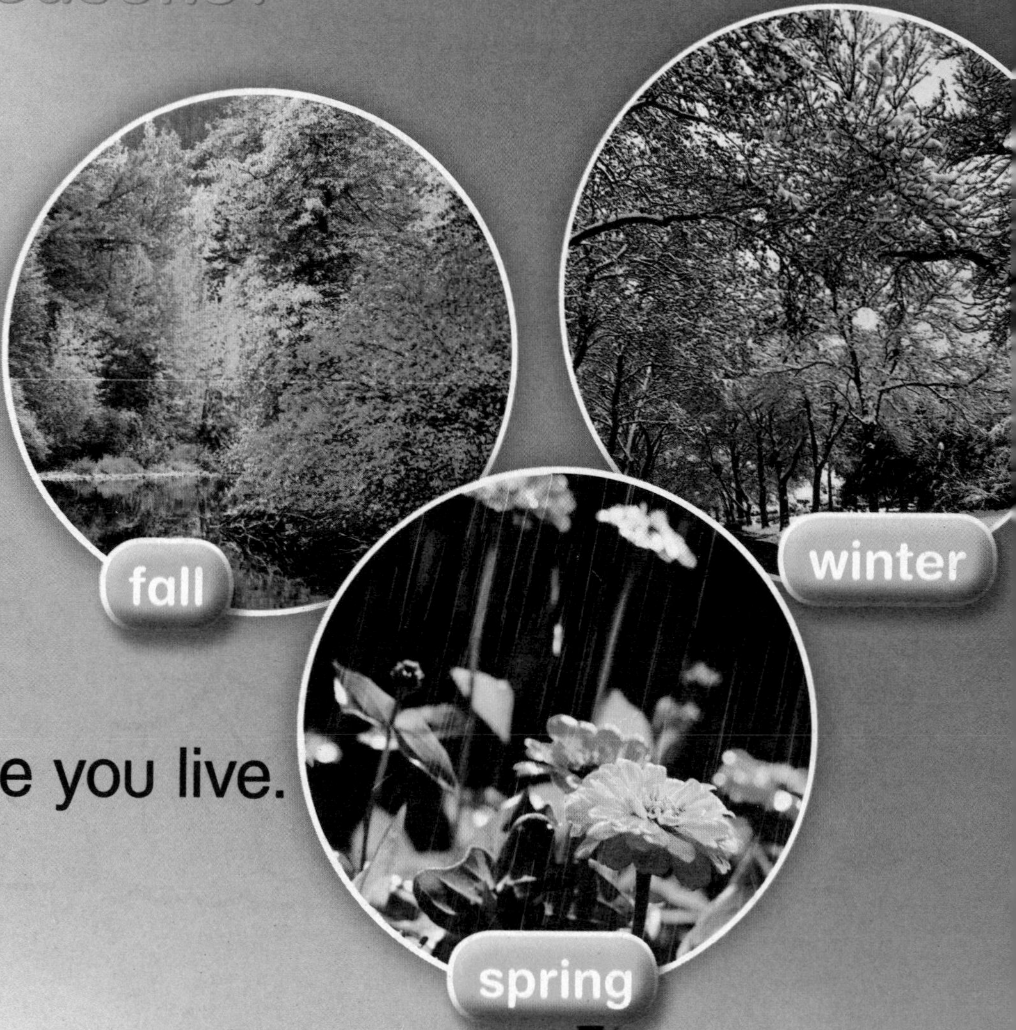
fall
winter
spring

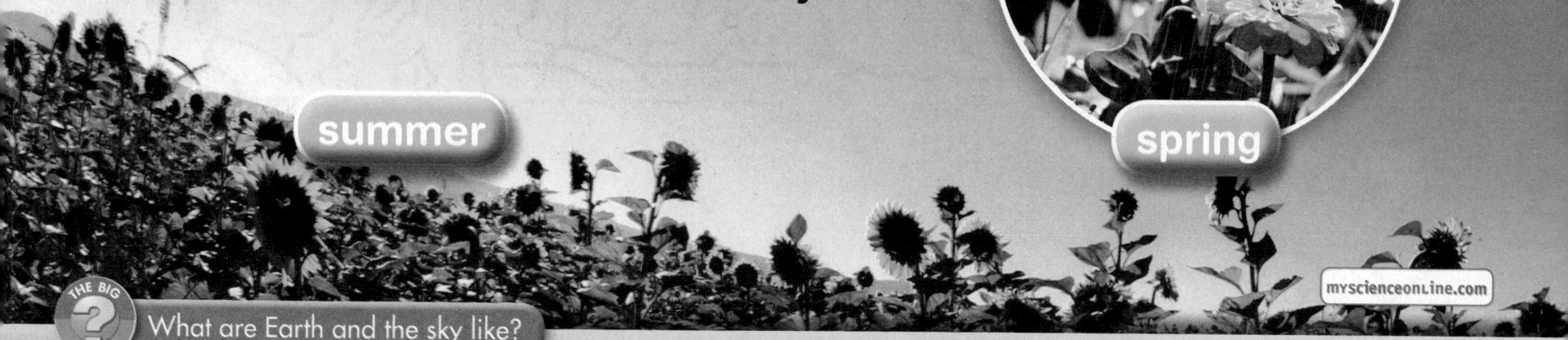
summer
myscienceonline.com

THE BIG ? What are Earth and the sky like?

What are the seasons?

 Color the picture of winter blue.

Color the picture of summer yellow.

Color the picture of spring green.

Color the picture of fall red.

Activity 53
Use with page 53.

Directions: Discuss with children the seasons and different kinds of weather associated with each season. Have children color something in each seasonal picture with the color named for that season.

Home Activity: Discuss with your child how your region is affected by the seasons. Then help your child draw a picture showing a favorite season.

What do the day and night skies look like?

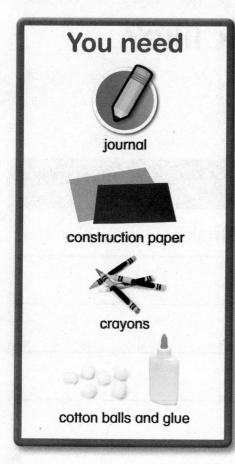

You need

journal

construction paper

crayons

cotton balls and glue

1 Label.

2 Make.

3 Compare.

4 Write.

What is in the sky?

Object	Day	Night

Day

Night

myscienceonline.com

Name _____

What do the day and night skies look like?

 **Draw.**

Compare.

Objects in the Sky		
Object	**Day**	**Night**

Activity 54
Use with page 54.

 Directions: Have children draw their pictures in the "Object" column. Have them look at their pictures. Have them use check marks to show which objects are visible during the day, which are visible at night, and which are visible at both times.

RAIN | ICY | MIX | SNOW | SEVERE

Big World My World

Ready for the Weather

People learn about the weather across the country.

You learn about the weather too.

What do you do to get ready for rainy weather?

Big World

My World

Nashville 87 71

Charlotte 70

Atlanta

Austin

New Orleans 77

86 74 Orlando

87 79 Miami

mYscienceonLine.com

THE BIG ? What are Earth and the sky like?

55

Name _____

Ready for the Weather

Color the picture that shows what you could wear and use on a hot summer day.

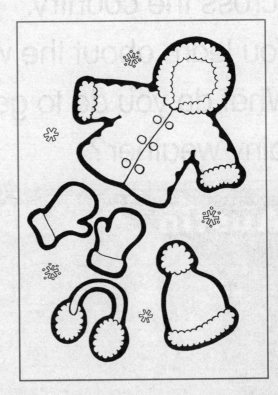

 **Directions:** Identify the items in each small picture, and have children color the picture with items that are most appropriate for a hot summer day.

 Home Activity: Watch or listen to a weather report with your child. Then choose clothes he or she might wear outdoors given the day's weather.

Physical Science

Unit D

Chapter 6
Objects

What are objects like?

Chapter 7
Matter and Mixtures

What are matter and mixtures?

Chapter 8
Motion

What are position and motion?

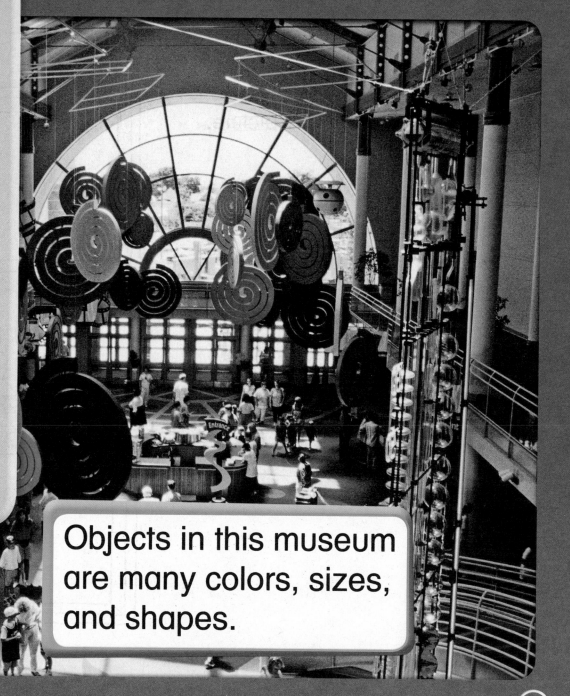

Objects in this museum are many colors, sizes, and shapes.

Name _____

Physical Science

 (Circle) the dinosaur in the picture.

Color the picture.

Directions: Discuss the picture with children. Ask children to circle the dinosaur on the page. Then have them color the picture. Discuss how the dinosaur and the other things on the page are all objects.

Home Activity: Your child is going to study physical science. He or she will learn about objects. Select an object in your home, such as a toy. Ask your child to tell about the object's shape, color, and size. Repeat with other items.

Objects

What do you see?

myscienceonline.com

Name _____

What are objects like?

Look at the pictures below.

(Circle) the pictures of things you
might find at a playground.

Draw a picture.

Show what you like to do at the
playground.

Activity 57
Use with page 57.

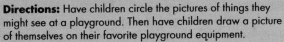

Directions: Have children circle the pictures of things they
might see at a playground. Then have children draw a picture
of themselves on their favorite playground equipment.

Home Activity: In Chapter 6, your child will learn about matter and its
properties. Point to an object in your home, and help your child describe
it by asking questions such as, "Is it big or little?" "Is it red or blue?"

How can you sort objects?

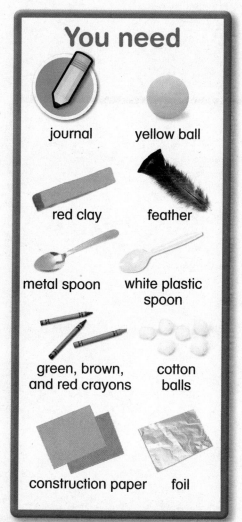

You need

journal

yellow ball

red clay

feather

metal spoon

white plastic spoon

green, brown, and red crayons

cotton balls

construction paper

foil

1 Look.

2 Touch.

3 Sort.

4 Write.

mysicienceonLine.com

Name ______________________________

Inquiry **Try It!**

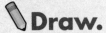

How can you sort objects?

Draw.

Activity 58
Use with page 58.

Directions: Have children draw a set of objects that are alike.

⊙ **Main Idea and Details**

This statue is a fountain.

The fountain sprays water.

The fountain has many colors.

Tell about the fountain.

THE BIG
? What are objects like?

myscienceonline.com

Name _____

Main Idea and Details

Color one boat green.

Color one boat red.

Color one boat brown.

Color the sun yellow.

Count the boats.

Write the number.

_____

- - - - - - - - - - - - - - - -

 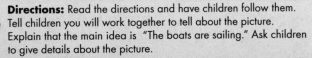 **Directions:** Read the directions and have children follow them. Tell children you will work together to tell about the picture. Explain that the main idea is "The boats are sailing." Ask children to give details about the picture.

 Home Activity: Tell your child how you use a room in your home. ("We use the kitchen to prepare and eat meals.") Ask your child to tell a detail about the room. Your child might say, "The kitchen has a stove." Encourage your child to give lots of details.

What are your five senses?

see

hear

smell

taste

touch

You have five senses. You use your senses to learn.

Name _____

What are your five senses?

 Draw a line to match each sense word with the correct picture.

 see   hear   smell   taste   touch

Directions: Read the sense words to children. Help them identify the pictures. Discuss which picture goes with each sense word. Have children draw lines to match the sense words with the appropriate pictures.

 Home Activity: Point to your eyes and say, "I use my eyes to _____." Have your child complete the sentence with the appropriate sense word: "I use my eyes to see." Continue with your ears, nose, mouth/tongue, and hands.

What are objects made of?

Objects are made of different things.

Some objects are made of wood.

Some objects are made of plastic.

Tell what the objects in the picture are made of.

What are objects made of?

(Circle) the object made of wood.

Color the picture.

Directions: Help children identify the objects the baseball players are holding. Then have them circle the object made of wood and color the picture.

Home Activity: Ask your child to find and name two objects made of wood in your home. Then ask them to name two objects made of plastic.

Lesson 3

What can you tell about objects?

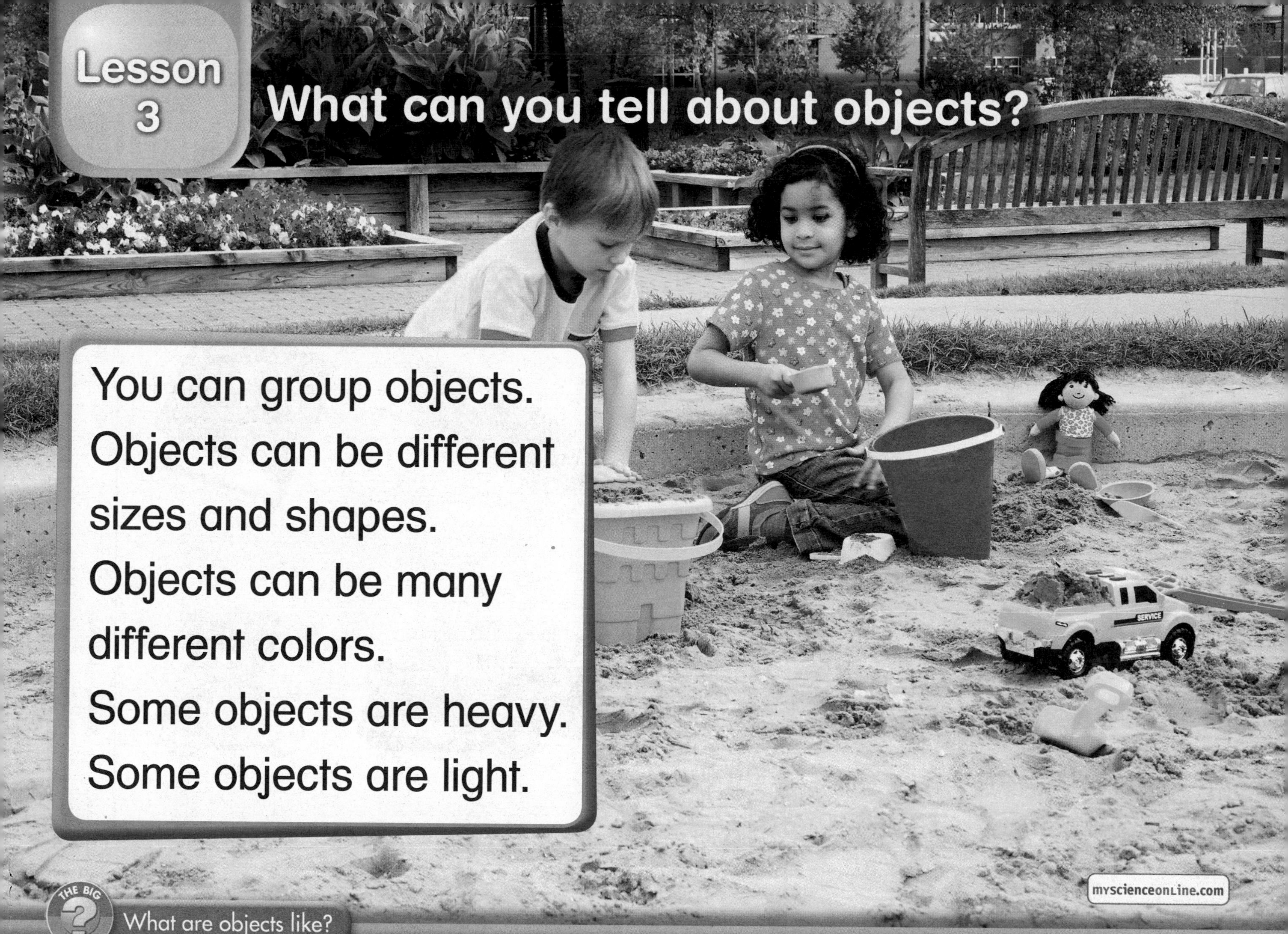

You can group objects.
Objects can be different sizes and shapes.
Objects can be many different colors.
Some objects are heavy.
Some objects are light.

THE BIG ? What are objects like?

myscienceonline.com

Name _____

What can you tell about objects?

Circle the things that are heavy.

Circle the things that are light.

Directions: Help children name the objects in the top box. Have them circle the heavy objects. Repeat the process for the bottom box, but ask children to circle the light objects.

Home Activity: Give your child an object, such as a dinner plate. Ask your child to describe the object using as many words as possible. Then have him or her tell whether the object is heavy or light.

How can you sort objects?

You can sort by size.

You can sort by weight.

You can sort by how objects feel.

THE BIG ? What are objects like?

myscienceonline.com

63

How can you sort objects?

 Color the biggest object in each picture.

 Activity 63 Use with page 63.

Directions: Remind children that one way to sort objects is by size. Help them identify the stacking dolls in the first picture and tell them to color the biggest one. Repeat the process for the other pictures.

Home Activity: Have fun sorting objects with your child. You might sort objects, such as books, by size. You might sort objects, such as balls, by weight. You might sort objects that are soft or hard.

Lesson 5

How can you use objects?

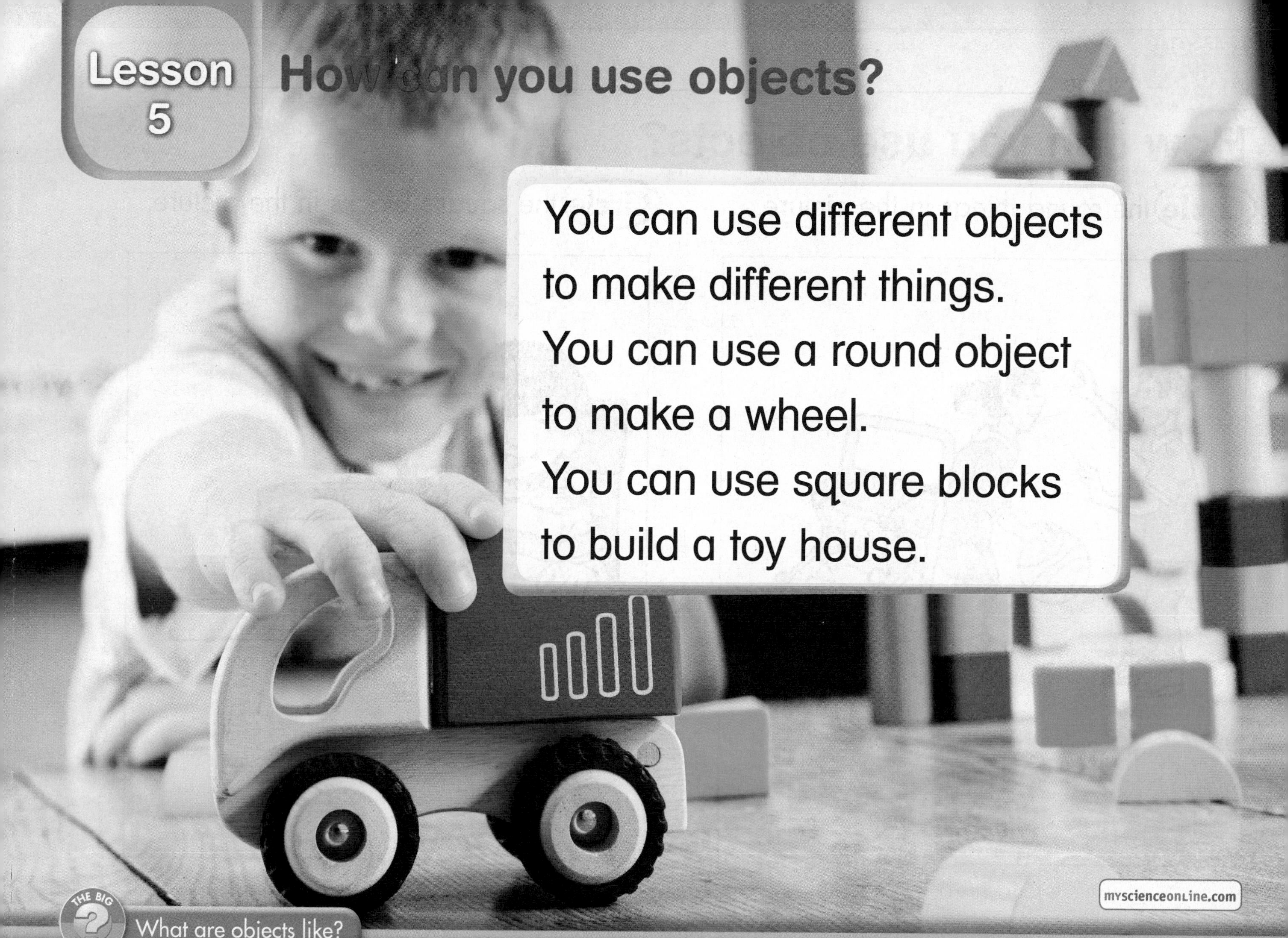

You can use different objects to make different things.
You can use a round object to make a wheel.
You can use square blocks to build a toy house.

myscienceonline.com

THE BIG ? What are objects like?

How can you use objects?

Circle the round things in the picture.

Circle the square blocks in the picture.

Activity 64
Use with page 64.

Directions: Have children circle the round objects in the first picture. Discuss how the shape of the round objects make them useful as balls and wheels. Then ask children to circle the square shapes in the second picture. Discuss why blocks with square shapes are good for building.

Home Activity: Help your child identify round things in and around your home and tell how they are used. Then find square things and tell how they are used.

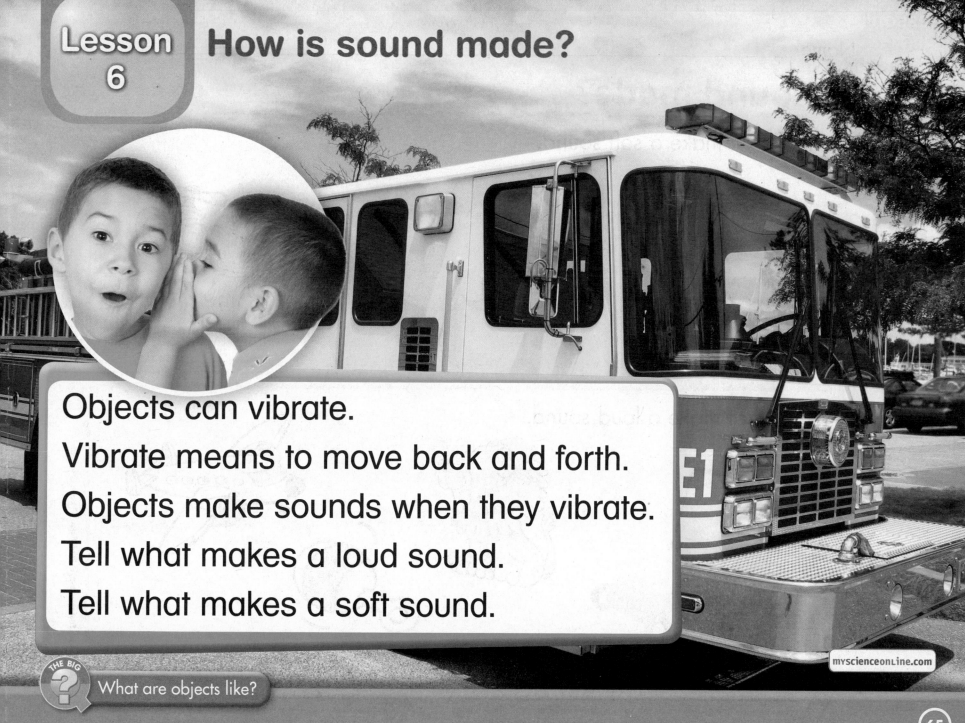

Lesson 6

How is sound made?

Objects can vibrate.

Vibrate means to move back and forth.

Objects make sounds when they vibrate.

Tell what makes a loud sound.

Tell what makes a soft sound.

THE BIG ? What are objects like?

myscienceonLine.com

65

How is sound made?

Circle the things that make a soft sound.

  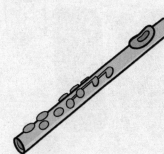 

Circle the things that make a loud sound.

 Activity 65 Use with page 65.

 Directions: Have children identify the pictures in the first box. Ask which pictures show things that make soft sounds. Have children circle those things. Proceed in the same way with the second set of pictures, asking children to identify and circle things that make loud sounds.

 Home Activity: Have your child identify loud and soft sounds that you might hear at home. For example, a ticking clock makes a soft sound, but a truck rumbling down the street might make a loud sound.

Which object is heavier?

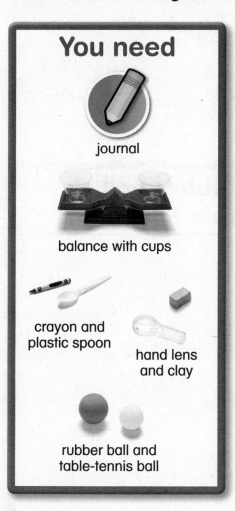

You need

journal

balance with cups

crayon and
plastic spoon

hand lens
and clay

rubber ball and
table-tennis ball

1 Put.

2 Look.

3 Write.

4 Put.

5 Look.

THE BIG ? What are objects like?

Name _____

Which object is heavier?

Look. Which is heavier?

**Draw.**

Crayon or Spoon	Hand Lens or Clay	Rubber Ball or Table Tennis Ball

Directions: Have children place the items in the cups on the balance, then draw the item that is heavier.

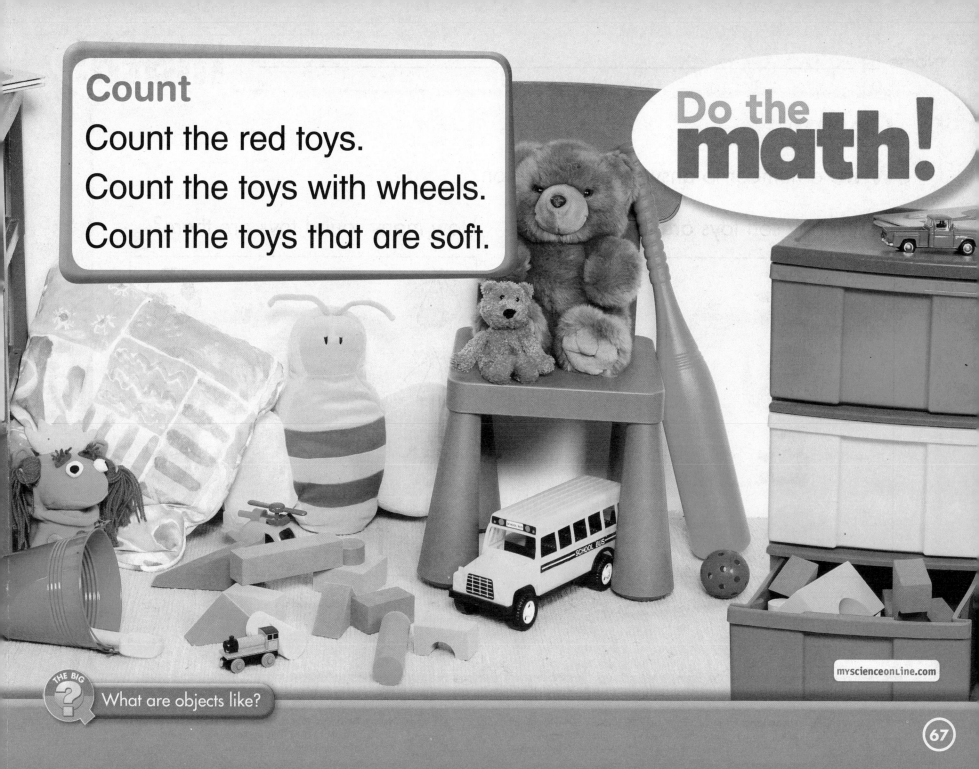

Count

Count the red toys.

Count the toys with wheels.

Count the toys that are soft.

Do the math!

myscienceonline.com

Name _____

Do the math!

Count

 Write a number to answer each question.

How many soft toys are there?

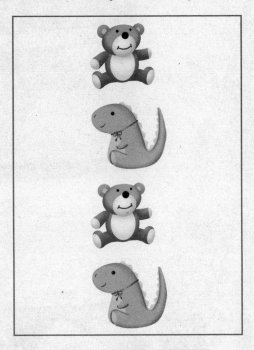

_ _ _ _ _ _ _ _ _ _ _ _ _ _ _ _

_ _ _ _ _ _ _ _ _ _ _ _ _ _ _ _

How many round toys are there?

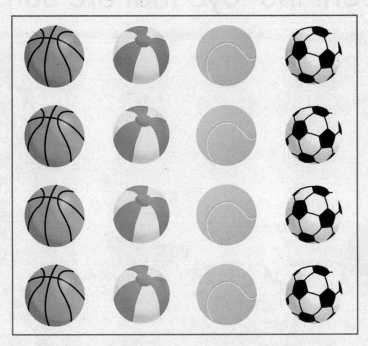

_ _ _ _ _ _ _ _ _ _ _ _ _ _ _ _

_ _ _ _ _ _ _ _ _ _ _ _ _ _ _ _

Activity 67
Use with page 67.

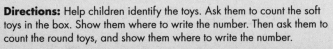
Directions: Help children identify the toys. Ask them to count the soft toys in the box. Show them where to write the number. Then ask them to count the round toys, and show them where to write the number.

Home Activity: Your child has learned how to count groups of objects that are alike. Line up items, such as pennies, on a table. Have your child count the items.

Chapter **7**

Matter and Mixtures

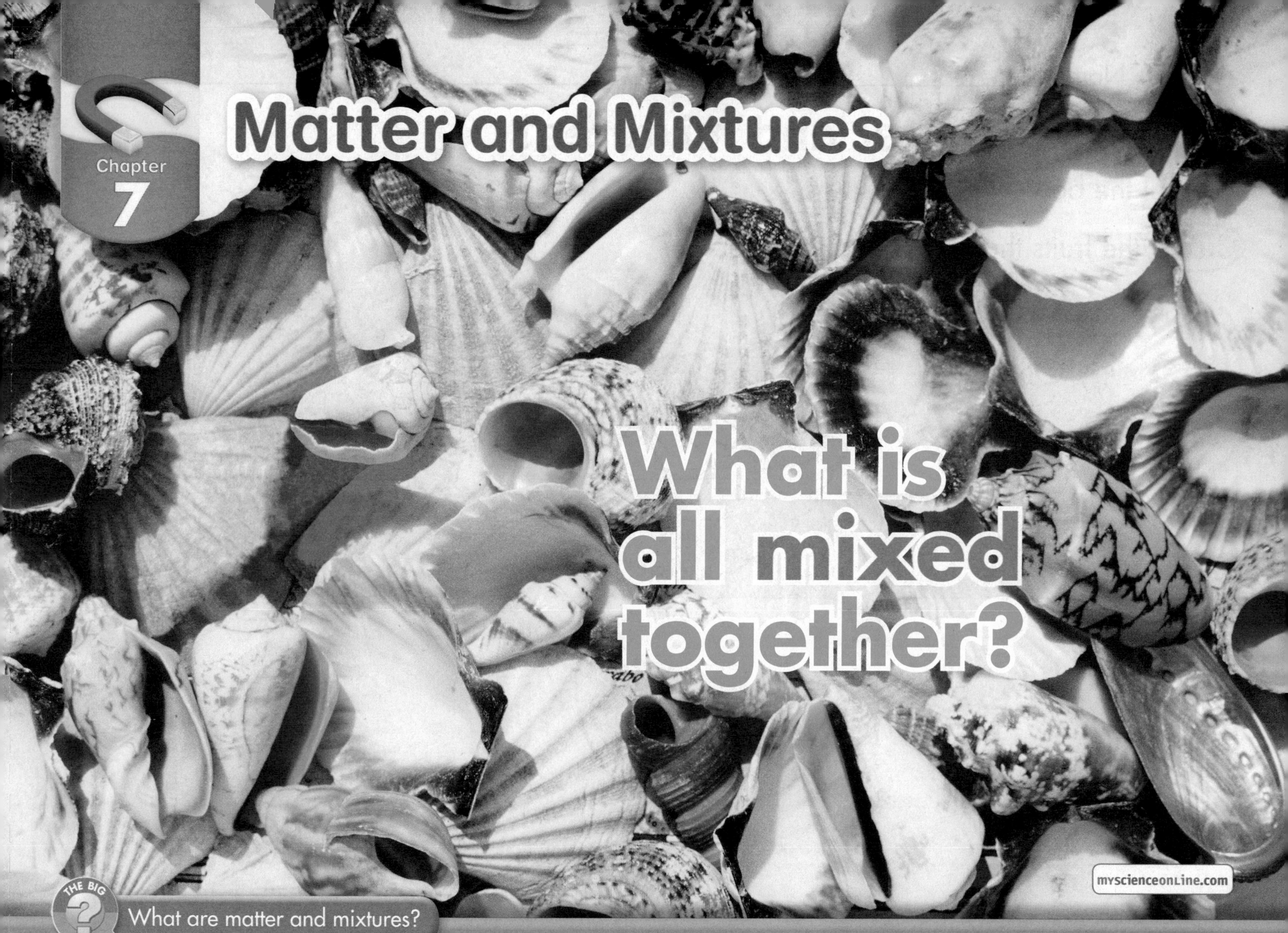

What is all mixed together?

THE BIG

? What are matter and mixtures?

Name _____

What are matter and mixtures?

Look at the bowl.

Circle the fruits that are mixed together.

 Directions: Help children identify the fruit in the bowl. Then have children circle the fruit they recognize from the bowl.

 Home Activity: With your child, identify mixtures in the kitchen, such as granola or salad. Talk about how mixtures are made of many parts mixed together, and identify the parts that make up your kitchen mixtures.

How do materials change?

You need

journal

paper

clay

scissors

1 Cut.

Crumple.

2 Scrunch.

Stretch.

3 Tear.

Twist.

4 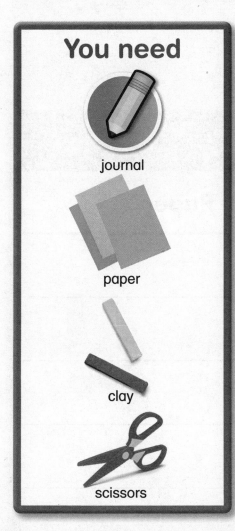 Draw.

myscienceonline.com

Name _____

Inquiry **Try It!**

How do materials change?

Write.

Did It Change?		
	Clay	**Paper**
Shape		
Size		
Feel		
Color		
Material		

Activity 69
Use with page 69.

Directions: Have children fold, flatten, scrunch, stretch, and rip clay and paper. Then have them record (*Yes or No*) whether the clay and paper changed in the ways listed on the table.

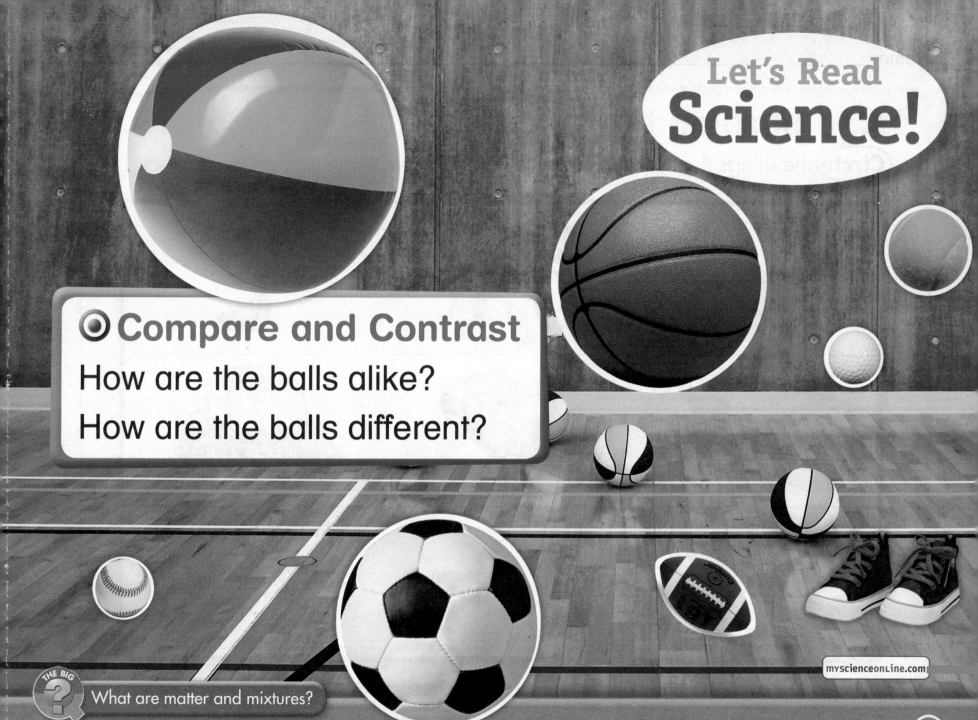

◎**Compare and Contrast**

How are the balls alike?

How are the balls different?

THE BIG ? What are matter and mixtures?

myscienceonline.com

Name _____

Compare and Contrast

(Circle) the things that belong together in each row.

 Directions: Help children identify the pictures in each row. Then have them circle the two things that are most alike in each row.

 **Home Activity:** Place groups of similar objects, such as art supplies, together. Have your child identify how the objects are alike. Then introduce a new object and have your child tell whether it belongs.

The children measure a block castle.

A block is a solid.

Solids keep their shape.

Name other things that are solids.

Tell what you observe about the solids.

THE BIG ? What are matter and mixtures?

myscienceonline.com

71

Name _____

What are solids like?

 Draw an ✕ in the box if the object keeps its shape.

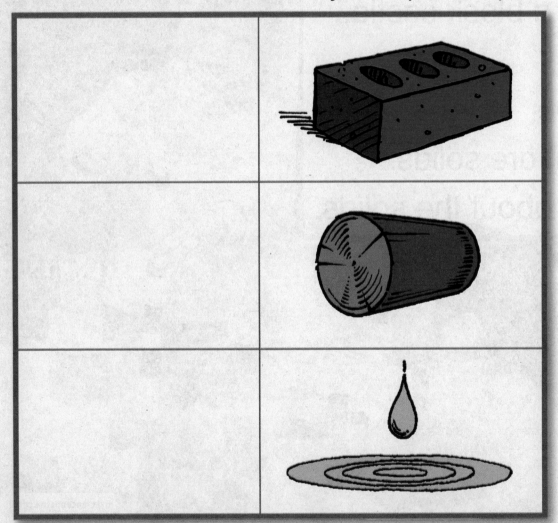

 **Directions:** Remind children that an object that keeps its shape is a solid. Then have children write an X in the box next to solid objects.

 Home Activity: Ask your child to identify objects in the room that are solids. Be sure to have at least one nonsolid, such as water in a vase or glass, in the room. Ask your child if the water is a solid. If needed, explain that it is not a solid. It does not keep its shape.

What are liquids like?

Water is a liquid.
Liquids take the shape
of their containers.
Name other liquids.

THE BIG ? What are matter and mixtures?

myscienceonLine.com

72

Name _____

What are liquids like?

 **Color** the part of the picture that is liquid.

 Directions: Have children identify what the girl is doing with the faucet and connect it to what they have learned about liquids. Then have them color the liquids pictured.

 Home Activity: Fill a pitcher with water or juice and pour some of the liquid into a cup to demonstrate that liquids take the shape of their containers. Discuss with your child ways that your family uses liquids every day.

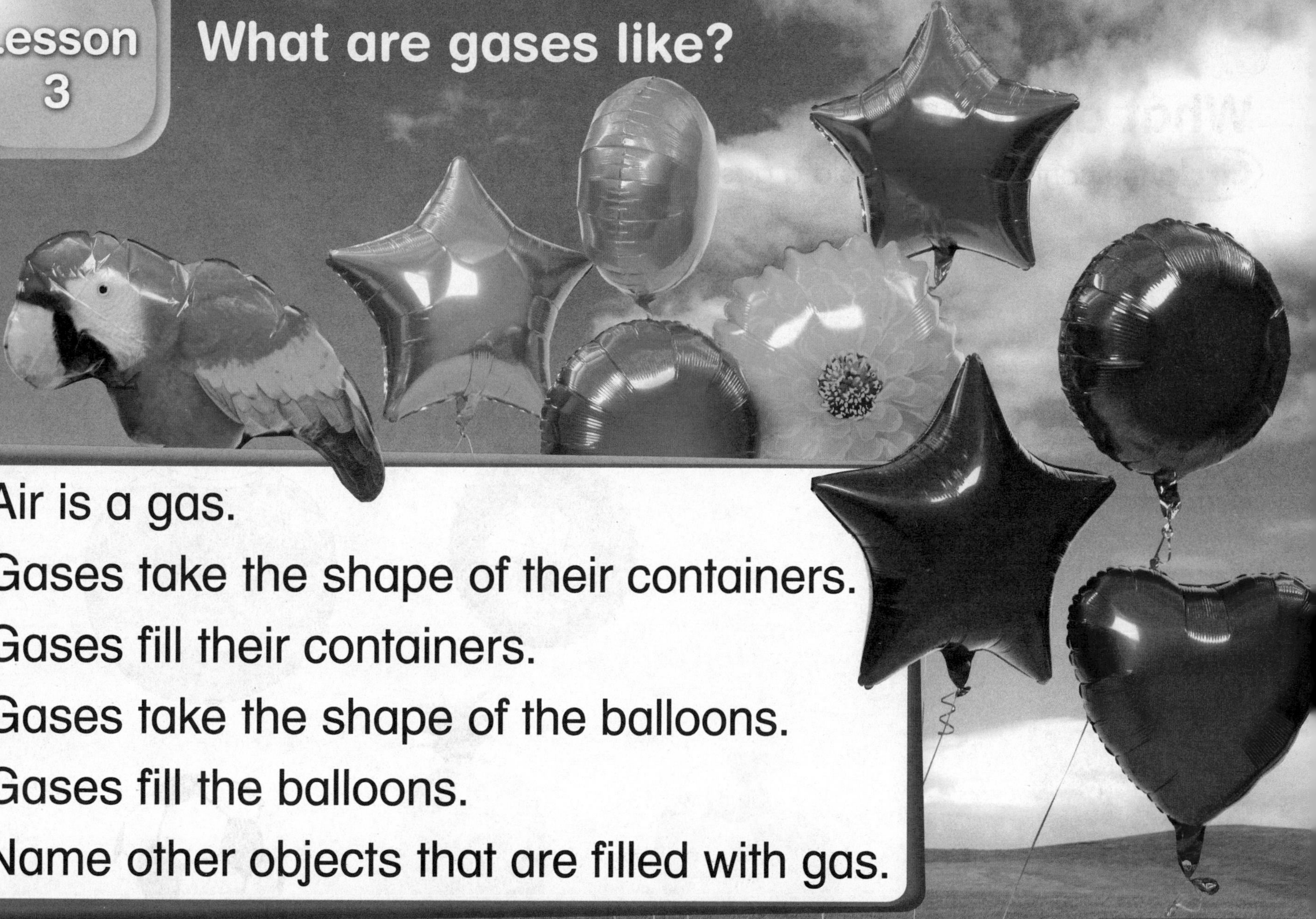

Air is a gas.

Gases take the shape of their containers.

Gases fill their containers.

Gases take the shape of the balloons.

Gases fill the balloons.

Name other objects that are filled with gas.

THE BIG

What are matter and mixtures?

myscienceonline.com

What are gases like?

(Circle) the containers that hold a gas.

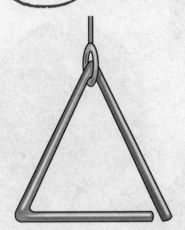

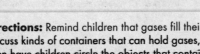

Directions: Remind children that gases fill their containers. Discuss kinds of containers that can hold gases, such as balloons. Then have children circle the objects that contain a gas.

Home Activity: Point to objects in your home and ask your child if the item contains a gas. For example, kitchen containers with closed lids may have air in them, but they cannot hold a gas if the lid is not on.

How can water change?

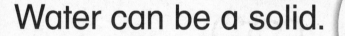

Water can be a solid.

Ice is solid water.

Ice can melt.

It changes from a solid to a liquid.

Water can boil.

It changes from a liquid to a gas.

THE BIG

What are matter and mixtures?

myscienceonline.com

74

How can water change?

Color the picture that shows water changing.

Activity 74
Use with page 74.

Directions: Discuss with children the different forms of water shown. Explain the terms *melt* and *boil* if needed. Have children identify and color the picture that shows a change.

Home Activity: Show your child ice changing into water. Fill a glass with ice. Watch as the ice melts.

Lesson 5

What is a mixture?

You can put things together to make a mixture.

Look at the pictures.

Tell what is mixed together.

Name other mixtures.

Tell what makes up those mixtures.

What is a mixture?

Make a mixture of flowers.

Draw different flowers together in the vase.

 **Directions:** Have children draw flowers of their choosing in the empty vase. Then discuss with them how their picture shows a mixture.

 Home Activity: Find mixtures around the home and help your child identify the components of the mixtures. Let the mixtures range from the familiar (trail mix) to the unfamiliar (the contents of a toolbox).

What is in a mixture?

You need

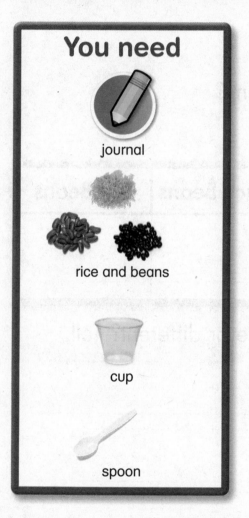

journal

rice and beans

cup

spoon

1 Count.
Write.
Mix.

2 Group.

3 Count.
Write.
Compare.

Name _____

What is in a mixture?

Count. How many?

 **Write.**

Rice	Black Beans	Red Beans

Mix.

Group.

Count. How many?

Write.

Rice	Black Beans	Red Beans

Are they the same or different? Tell.

_____

_____

_____

 **Activity 76**
Use with page 76.

Directions: Have children count the red beans, black beans, and rice grains and write down the number. Then tell them to mix the three piles together in a plastic cup. After they have created a mixture, have children put their rice, red beans, and black beans into three groups. Tell children to count how many grains of rice, black beans, and red beans are in each pile and then write down the number. Ask children if the numbers are the same or different.

Food Mixtures

You eat many mixtures.

Breakfast cereal and milk are a mixture.

List the foods you and your family like.

Tell which ones are mixtures.

THE BIG ? What are matter and mixtures?

mysclenceonLine.com

Food Mixtures

(Circle) two or more foods to mix in a soup.

 Then **draw** the food you circled in the bowl.

 Directions: Identify the food shown in each box. Then have children circle two or more foods to mix in a soup. Have them draw the foods they circled in the soup bowl.

 Home Activity: With your child, keep a list of food mixtures you enjoy during one meal of the day.

Motion

How does the ball move?

THE BIG **?**

What are position and motion?

myscienceonline.com

Name _____

What are position and motion?

Look at each picture.

Circle the person who made the ball move.

 Draw an arrow where you think the ball will go.

 Activity 78
Use with page 78.

Directions: Discuss how each picture shows a ball in motion. Then have children circle the person who made the ball move in the first picture. Guide them in using the motion lines to help predict where the ball will go. Have them draw an arrow to show their prediction. Repeat the procedure for the second picture.

 Home Activity: Demonstrate different types of motion using a ball. Toss, kick, and roll a ball back and forth with your child.

How do objects move?

You need

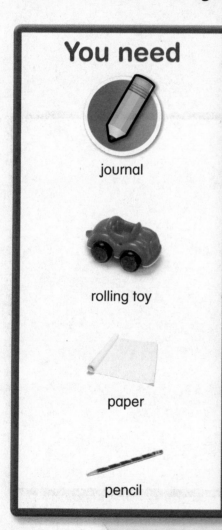

journal

rolling toy

paper

pencil

1 Move.

2 Trace.

3 Observe.

4 Draw.

Name _____

How do objects move?

 Draw how objects move.

Directions: Have children roll a ball or push a toy across a solid surface and draw what happens when the ball rolls away from them.

⊙ Cause and Effect

What made the swing move?

What are position and motion?

myscienceonline.com

Name _____

Let's Read
Science!

Cause and Effect

Look at what happened in each row.

Circle the picture that shows why it happened.

Activity 80
Use with page 80.

Directions: Tell children that the first picture in each row shows what has happened. Have children tell what they see in the first picture in row 1. Then have children circle the picture that shows why the balloon is in the air. Continue in the same way for rows 2 and 3.

Home Activity: Demonstrate examples of cause-and-effect relationships in the home. For example, dirty dishes get clean because they are washed, and a light turns off because you flick a switch.

What can you tell about an object's position?

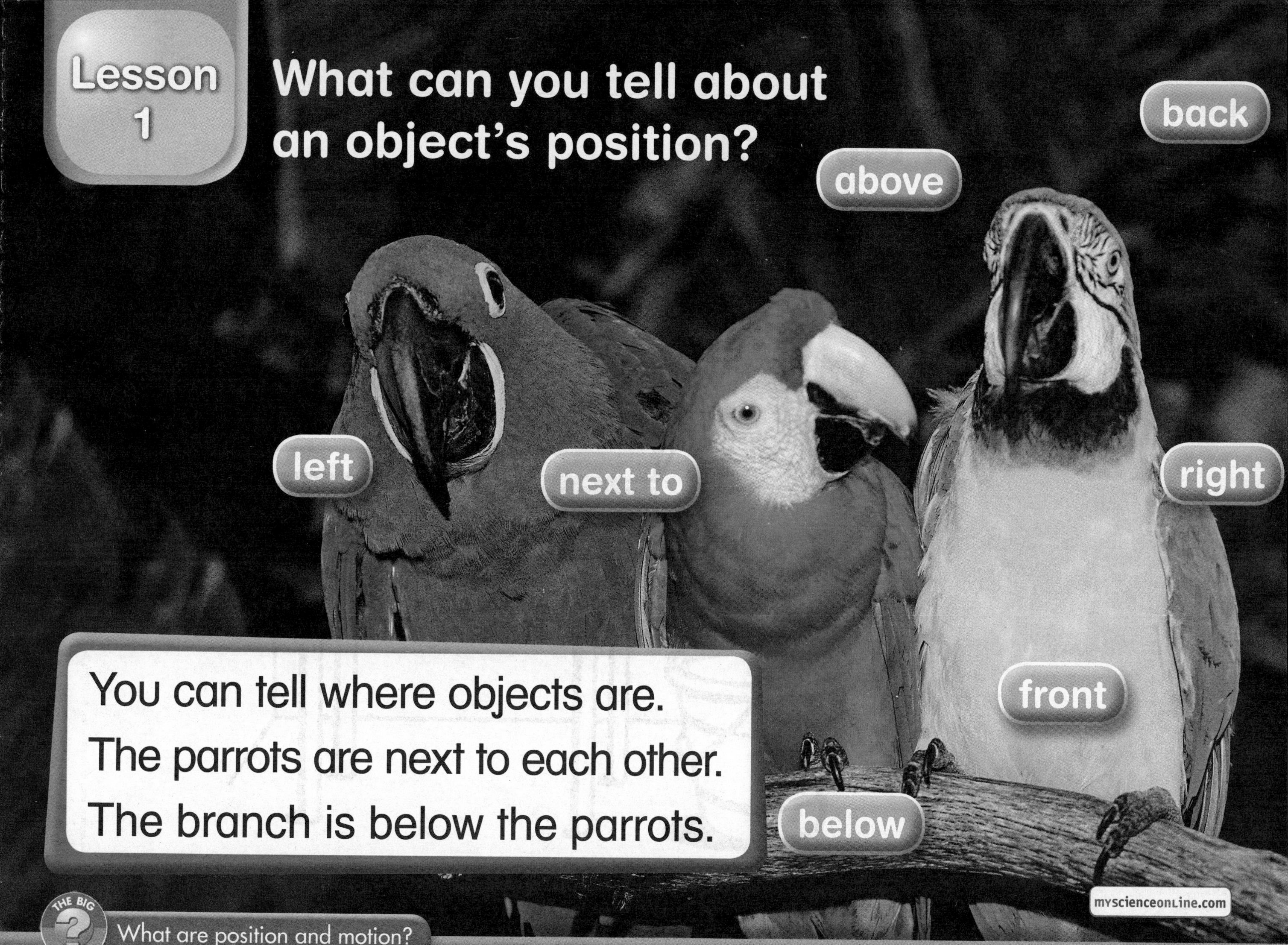

back

above

left

next to

right

front

You can tell where objects are.

The parrots are next to each other.

The branch is below the parrots.

below

 What are position and motion?

mysCienceonLine.com

What can you tell about an object's position?

 Draw an ✗ on the object next to the table.

 Color the object below the pitcher.

Directions: Discuss with children the position of the objects in the picture. Guide them in understanding the relationships between *above/below*, *front/back*, and *right/left*. Then have children identify the table, pitcher, spool of thread, and the bucket.

Home Activity: Use household objects to help your child practice identifying position. Point to an object and ask your child to describe its position relative to another object. For example, point to an overhead light and ask if the light is above or below the table.

What makes objects move?

You can use a push to move an object.
You can use a pull to move an object.
A push or a pull can change how
an object moves.

What are position and motion?

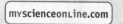
82

Name _____

What makes objects move?

Circle pictures that show a push.

 Draw an ✗ on pictures that show a pull.

 **Activity 82**
Use with page 82.

Directions: Have children identify each picture and tell whether it shows a push or a pull. Then have children circle pictures showing pushes and put an X on pictures showing pulls.

 Home Activity: Have your child use a toy to demonstrate pushes and pulls.

What are some ways objects move?

Objects may move fast or slowly.
Look at these objects.
Put the objects in order from slowest to fastest.

THE BIG ? What are position and motion?

myscienceonline.com

Name _____

What are some ways objects move?

Color things that move fast blue.

Color things that move slowly red.

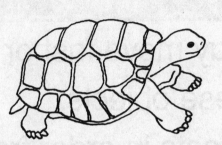

Directions: Discuss *fast* and *slow* as opposites. Then have children identify and color the animals, objects, and people that move fast blue and those that move slowly red.

Home Activity: Play an outdoors speed game with your child. Name something that moves fast, such as a train, and have your child run. Continue by naming fast- and slow-moving things and having your child run or walk to show how each thing moves.

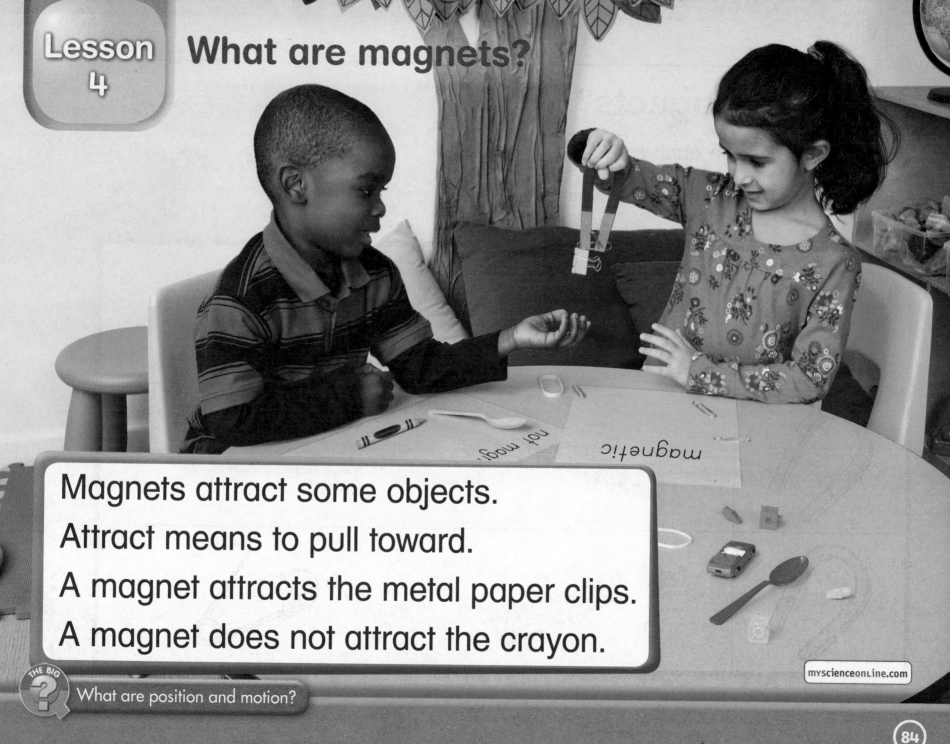

What are magnets?

not magnetic

magnetic

Magnets attract some objects.

Attract means to pull toward.

A magnet attracts the metal paper clips.

A magnet does not attract the crayon.

myscienceonline.com

THE BIG ? What are position and motion?

84

What are magnets?

Look at the objects in each row.

(Circle) the one that the magnet will attract.

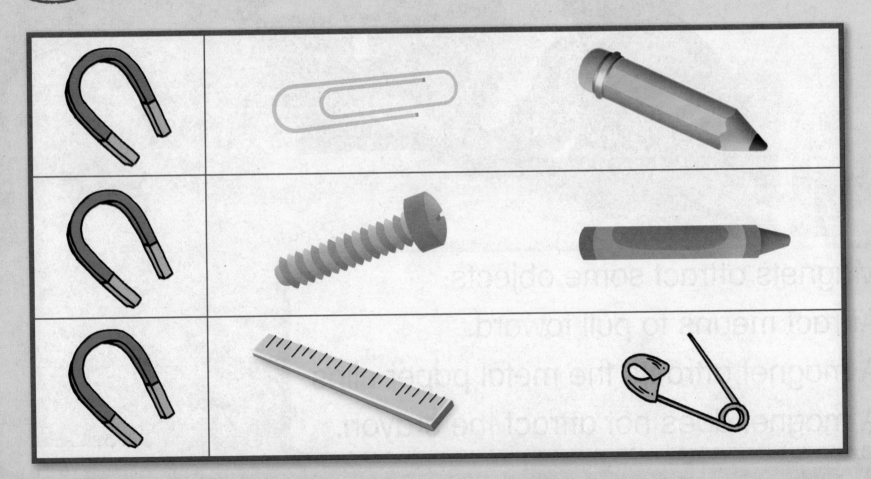

 Directions: Discuss with children different objects and metal materials that magnets attract. Then have them circle the object in each row that the magnet would attract.

 Home Activity: With your child, use a refrigerator magnet to test household objects for magnetism. Help your child record how objects react to the magnet.

Inquiry **Investigate It!**

How can you move the car?

You need

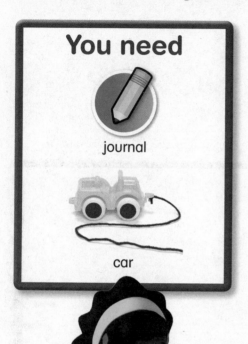

journal

car

1 Push.

Push hard.

Tell.

2 Pull.

Pull hard.

Tell.

3 Draw.

myscienceonline.com

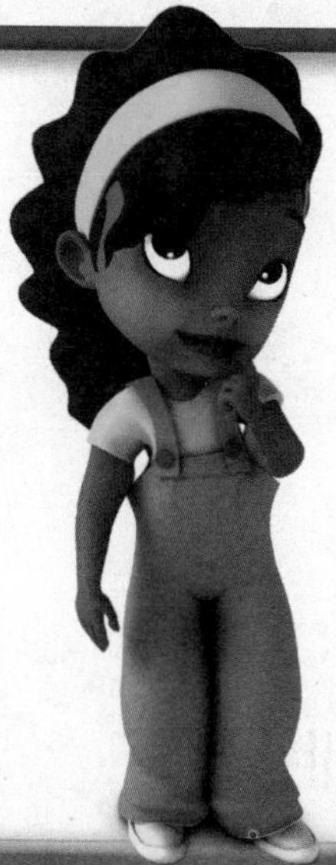

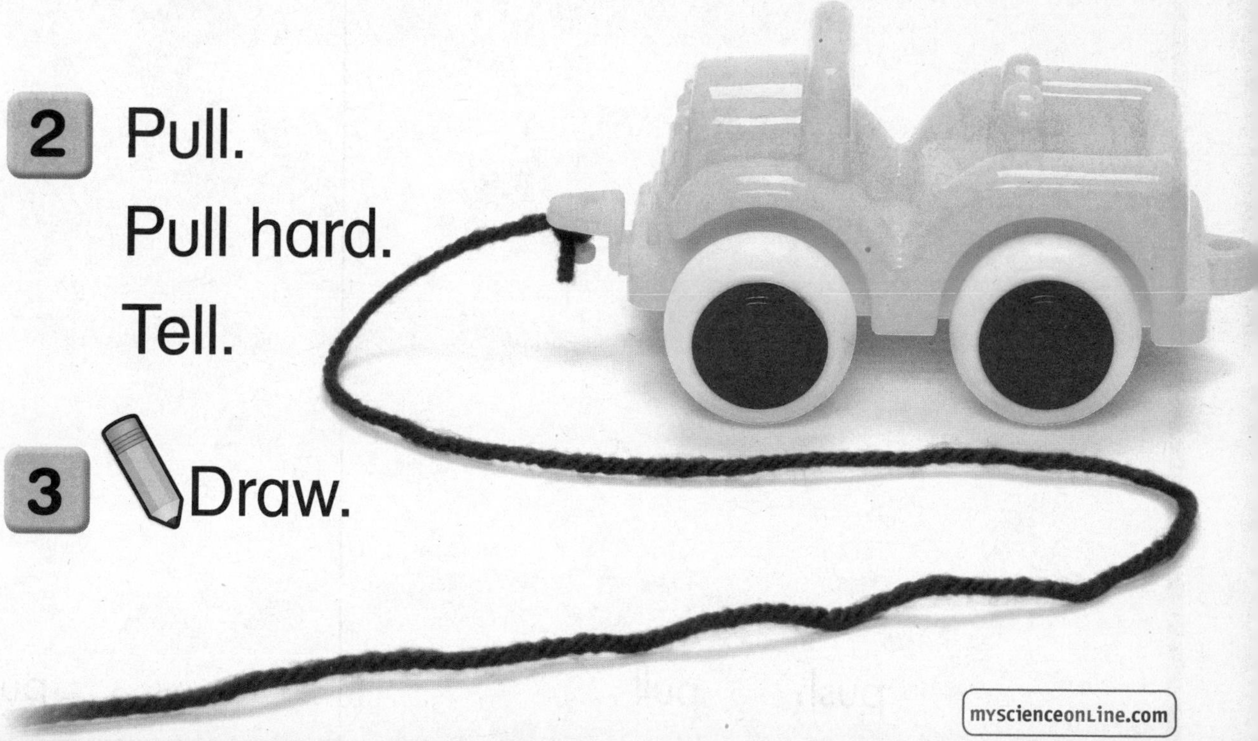

Name ____________________

Inquiry **Investigate It!**

How can you move the car?

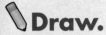

Draw.

Circle push or pull.

push pull	push pull

Activity 85
Use with page 85.

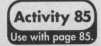

Directions: Have children draw a hand pushing the car and then circle *push*. Have children draw a hand pulling the car and then circle *pull*.

STEM

Slide Engineer

Slides can be made by engineers.

The engineer uses math.

The engineer uses technology.

The engineer makes the slide fun.

The engineer makes the slide safe.

THE BIG
?
What are position and motion?

myscienceonLine.com

Science
Technology
Engineering
Math

Slide Engineer

STEM

✎ **Draw** a plan to build a slide.

 Activity 86
Use with page 86.

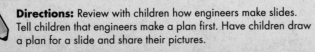 **Directions:** Review with children how engineers make slides. Tell children that engineers make a plan first. Have children draw a plan for a slide and share their pictures.

 Home Activity: Talk with your child about things you plan around the house, such as what to make for dinner. Plan a household task with your child. Have your child assist in writing or drawing your plan.

Credits

Staff Credits

The people who made up the *Interactive Science* team—representing composition services, core design digital and multimedia production services, digital product development, editorial, editorial services, manufacturing, and production—are listed below.

Geri Amani, Alisa Anderson, Jose Arrendondo, Amy Austin, David Bailis, Scott Baker, Lindsay Bellino, Charlie Bink, Bridget Binstock, Holly Blessen, Robin Bobo, Craig Bottomley, Jim Brady, Laura Brancky, Chris Budzisz, Odette Calderon, Sitha Chhor, Mary Chingwa, Caroline Chung, Margaret Clampitt, Kier Cline, Brandon Cole, Mitch Coulter, AnnMarie Coyne, Fran Curran, Dana Damiano, Michael Di Maria, Nancy Duffner, Amanda Ferguson, David Gall, Mark Geyer, Amy Goodwin, Gerardine Griffin, Chris Haggerty, Margaret Hall, Laura Hancko, Christian Henry, Autumn Hickenlooper, Guy Huff, George Jacobson, Marian Jones, Kathi Kalina, Chris Kammer, Sheila Kanitsch, Alyse Kondrat, Mary Kramer, Thea Limpus, Dominique Mariano, Lori McGuire, Melinda Medina, Angelina Mendez, Claudi Mimo, John Moore, Kevin Mork, Chris Niemyjski, Phoebe Novak, Anthony Nuccio, Jeff Osier, Charlene Rimsa, Rebecca Roberts, Camille Salerno, Manuel Sanchez, Carol Schmitz, Amanda Seldera, Sheetal Shah, Jeannine Shelton El, Geri Shulman, Greg Sorenson, Samantha Sparkman, Mindy Spelius, Karen Stockwell, Dee Sunday, Dennis Tarwood, Jennie Teece, Lois Teesdale, Michaela Tudela, Karen Vuchichevich, Barbara Watters, Tom Wickland, James Yagelski, Tim Yetzina, Diane Zimmermann

Illustrations

ACT1, ACT33, ACT62, ACT68 Ron Berg; **ACT4, ACT13, ACT65, ACT68** Bob Ostrom; **ACT4, ACT5, ACT6, ACT9, ACT20, ACT23, ACT24, ACT26, ACT29, ACT32, ACT33, ACT36, ACT40, ACT48, ACT49, ACT57, ACT65, ACT84** Jenny B Harris; **ACT4, ACT9, ACT12, ACT18, ACT20, ACT62, ACT70, ACT73, ACT80, ACT84** Ken Gamage; **ACT4, ACT12, ACT20, ACT65, ACT75** Remy Simard; **ACT5, ACT12, ACT13, ACT48, ACT49, ACT51, ACT77** John Haslam;

ACT5, ACT26, ACT29, ACT41, ACT73 Paul Sharp; **ACT5, ACT12, ACT24, ACT26, ACT29, ACT33, ACT67, ACT70, ACT73, ACT84** Robin Boyer; **ACT6, ACT18, ACT26, ACT33, ACT38, ACT39, ACT40, ACT49, . ACT65, ACT68, ACT70, ACT77, ACT80** Chris Lensch; **ACT6, ACT40, ACT48, ACT50** Julia Woolf; **ACT9, ACT57, ACT84** Jim Steck; **ACT9, ACT12, ACT13, ACT18, ACT70** Leslie Harrington; **ACT9, ACT12, ACT80** Michael Moran; **ACT12, ACT23** Holli Conger; **ACT24, ACT32, ACT67, ACT73** Luciana Navarro Powell; **ACT24, ACT73** Sheree Boyd; **ACT26, ACT49, ACT51** Sam Ward; **ACT26, ACT40** Scott Burroughs; **ACT32, ACT65** Jackie Stafford; **ACT57, ACT75** Brenda Sexton; **ACT62** Dean MacAdam; **ACT62** Geoffrey Paul Smith; **ACT73, ACT77** Christine Schneider; **ACT80** Chris Boyd.

Photographs

Every effort has been made to secure permission and provide appropriate credit for photographic material. The publisher deeply regrets any omission and pledges to correct errors called to its attention in subsequent editions.

Unless otherwise acknowledged, all photographs are the property of Pearson Education, Inc.

Photo locators denoted as follows: Top (T), Center (C), Bottom (B), Left (L), Right (R), Background (Bkgd)

Cover

William Gottlieb/Corbis

1 JGI/Jamie Grill/Getty Images; 2 Photolibrary Group, Inc.; 4 (T) ©Masterfile Royalty-Free; 5 ©Ian Scott/Shutterstock; 6 (BL) ©GAmut Stock Images Pvt Ltd Gamut/Alamy, (TR) ©PhotoAlto/Alamy, (BR) ©Westend61 GmbH/Alamy, (TL) Getty Images; 9 (TR) Image Source/Getty Images; 10 (Bkgrd) ©Shannon Fagan/Getty Images; 12 Christen Wooley; 15 DKCenteraTest/©DK Images; 16 (R) ©Fancy Collection/SuperStock; 17 (Bkgrd) ©Asia Images Group/Getty Images, (BL) Serhiy Kobyakov/123RF; 18 (R, L, C) ©Anton Vengo/SuperStock; 20 ©Blend Images/SuperStock, (Inset) ©Frank Miller/Time & Life Pictures/Getty Images; 22 ©Frank Cezus/Getty Images;

23 ©Big Cheese Photo/Jupiter Images; 25 (BL) ©Chris Hepburn/Getty Images, (Bkgrd) ©image100/Jupiter Images, (TL) ©Kenneth Jones/Alamy, (BR) ©Shem Compion/Getty Images, (TCR) ©WaterFrame/Alamy; 26 Cultura RM/Alamy Images; 27 ©Pierre Rosberg/Getty Images; 28 (Inset) Ole/Shutterstock, ©Keren Su/Getty Images; 29 (BCL) ©American Images Inc/Getty Images, (TCR) ©Frans Lemmens/Corbis, (BL) ©Leighton Photography & Imaging/Shutterstock, (TR) ©Rolf Nussbaumer/Nature Picture Library, (BR) Jupiter Images; 30 (BC) ©Casey K. Bishop/Shutterstock, (TR) ©Charlene Bayerle/Shutterstock, (Bkgrd) Photolibrary Group, Inc., (BL) Anekoho/Fotolia; 31 (BL) ©John Martin Will/Shutterstock, (TCL) ©Lisa a. Svara/Shutterstock, (TR) ©Steve Byland/Shutterstock; 32 ©Jeff Greenberg/Alamy Images; 33 ©James H. Robinson/Oxford Scientific/PhotoLibrary Group, Inc.; 35 ©iofoto/Shutterstock, (BR) ©Lilya/Shutterstock, (BL, BC) ©Ljupco Smokovski/Shutterstock, (BCR, BCL) Jane Burton/©DK Images; 36 (CL) ©Cathy Keifer/Shutterstock, (CR) ©Corbis/ Jupiter Images, (Bkgd) ©Gerard Lacz Images/SuperStock, (L) ©Masterfile Royalty-Free, (BR, BCL) ©Richard A. McGuirk/Shutterstock, (TR) Jupiter Images; 37 (Bkgrd) ©IKO/Shutterstock, (BL) ©Lisa a. Svara/Shutterstock, (BCL) ©Pieter/Shutterstock, (TCR, TCL, TC, BC) DK Images, (BC) Steve Shott/©DK Images; 38 (TC) ©DK Images, (TCR) ©Georgette Douwma/Getty Images, (TCL) ©marilyn barbone/Shutterstock, (Bkgrd) ©Purestock/Getty Images; 39 (TR, TL, TCR, TCL, C) Caroline Chung, (C, BR, BL, BCR, BCL) Manuel Sanchez; 40 ©blickwinkel/Alamy Images, ©Rolf Nussbaumer Photography/Alamy, ©sherwoodimagery/iStockphoto; 41 ©Bernd Neeser/Shutterstock, ©Kochneva Tetyana/Shutterstock, ©Leighton Photography & Imaging/Shutterstock, ©Tom Hirtreiter/Shutterstock, ©Tubuceo/Shutterstock; 43 (BR,) JSC/NASA; 44 ©Alexey Stiop/Shutterstock; 45 ©Jozsef Szasz-Fabian/Shutterstock; 47 ©Joe Fox/Alamy; 48 (TCL) ©Brand X Pictures/Getty Images, (BL) ©Digitaler Lumpensammier/Getty Images, (Bkgrd) ©joSon/Getty Images, (TR, BR) ©Jupiterimages/Getty Images, (TC) Leonello Calvetti/Stocktrek Images/Getty Images, (BC) ©123rf.com; 49 (TC) ©Datacraft/Getty Images, (Bkgrd) ©Doug

Chinnery/Getty Images, (BR) ©Steve Allen/Getty Images; 50 ©Galyna Andrushko/Shutterstock; 51 Photolibrary Group, Inc.; 52 ©Digitaler Lumpensammier/Getty Images; 53 (TR) ©Glen Allison/Getty Images, (TC) ©Purestock/Getty Images, (BC) ©Steve Satushek/Getty Images; 55 (Bkgrd) ©Dennis MacDonald/Alamy/Alamy Images, (Inset) Jupiter Images; 56 ©Mark Burnett/Alamy Images; 57 ©Jack Schiffer/Shutterstock; 59 ©claudio h. artman/Alamy; 63 Galina Barskaya/Shutterstock; 64 (Bkgrd) ©Heinrich van den Berg/Getty Images, ©Jupiterimages/Thinkstock; 65 (Bkgrd) Joy Brown/Shutterstock, (BCR) ©Tiplyashin Anatoly/Shutterstock, (Inset) Shutterstock; 68 ©bilderlounge/Tips RF/Jupiter Images; 70 (BR) ©Creative Crop/Getty Images, (Bkgrd) ©Felix Clinton/Getty Images, (BC) Corbis, (BR) Dave King/©DK Images, (TCL, CR) Getty Images, (TCR, C) Jupiter Images; 72 (BCL) ©laceybug/Shutterstock, (BR) ©Royalty-Free/Corbis, (BL) ©Thomas Del Brase/Getty Images, (BCR) Getty Images; 74 (Bkgrd) ©DK Images, (TR) ©George Hunter/SuperStock, (Inset) ©Image Source; 75 ©Nino Mascardi/Getty Images, (CR) ©Noam Armonn/Shutterstock; 77 ©Laura Johansen/Getty Images; 78 ©Ty Allison/Getty Images; 81 ©Sylvester Adams/Getty Images; 82 (BL) ©Liga Alksne/Shutterstock, (BC) ©Picsfive/Shutterstock, (BCR) ©SuperStock RF/SuperStock, (TR) Photolibrary Group, Inc.; 83 (TL) Marc Xavier/Fotolia, (Bkgd) Stefan Schurr/Shutterstock, (TCR) ©Ilja Masik/Shutterstock, (BCR) Mihai Cristian Saharia/Shutterstock, (BR) Thinkstock, (BL) Thinkstock; 86 Alamy Images; **BA1** ©Aleksi Markku/Shutterstock, ©Filipp Obada/Shutterstock, (TR) ©James Thew/Shutterstock, ©Jens Stolt/Shutterstock, Shutterstock.

About Science

Draw pictures. Write words.

_____

- -

_____

_____

- -

_____

_____

- -

_____

_____

- -

_____

About Science